ABOUT WORDPRESS EXPLAINED

You can build great websites with WordPress.

My name is Steve Burge, and I'm a full-time WordPress trainer. During thousands of WordPress classes in many cities and countries, I've met lots of different types of WordPress learners:

- WordPress learners come from many different backgrounds. They are accountants, florists, photographers, secretaries, factory workers, stay-at-home mothers and people from all walks of life. Two of our very best students have been a French teacher and a travel agent.

- WordPress learners don't need to know anything about websites. Some WordPress learners are professional web designers, but many others have never built a site before and don't know any website code or jargon.

- WordPress learners don't need any experience. We've trained people who went to work the previous week and found their boss saying "Surprise! You're running our WordPress site!" They often still wore their look of surprise.

- WordPress learners are of all ages. We've taught 15-year old students skipping class all the way up to retirees in their 80s.

If any of those descriptions sound like you, you've picked up the right book.

Using plain English and straightforward instructions, we'll enable you to build great websites using WordPress.

THIS BOOK IS ACTIVE

You don't learn to ride a bicycle by reading a book: you learn by actually riding.

You don't learn to drive a car by reading a book: you learn by actually driving.

A book will help and give some advice, but without actually riding a bike or driving a car, you'll never really learn. The same is true with WordPress. So throughout every chapter of this book, you're going to be asked to work with WordPress.

THIS BOOK USES SPECIFIC EXAMPLES

Once you've mastered the techniques in this book, you'll be able to build your own websites for companies, charities, schools, sports or whatever else you need.

However, in this book we're going to use a specific example site. Using specific examples makes it really easy to follow along together and know for certain that you're doing things right. At every step you'll have a clear screenshot to look at and compare with what you're seeing on your site. If it's not identical, you will easily know you've made a mistake, and you can try the steps one more time.

The example we're going to use is a city website. We're going to create a site with information about a fake city called Wordville. That's going to be the project we use to show you how to build and run a WordPress site.

By the end of the book, you will have built a site that looks like the image here:

Welcome to Wordville

Welcome to the website for the city of Wordville.

This is community where people love and use WordPress for their websites.

Recent Wordville News

Wordville Concert in the Park
WordCamp Europe in Belgrade
Join the Annual WordPress Events!
Welcome to Wordville

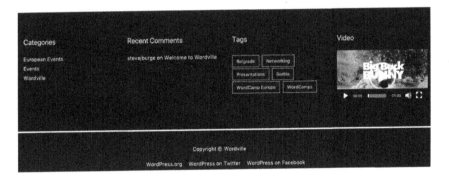

Categories

European Events
Events
Wordville

Recent Comments

stevejburge on Welcome to Wordville

Tags

Belgrade   Networking
Presentations   Serbia
WordCamp Europe   WordCamps

Video

00:00 ⬛━━━ 01:00 🔊 ⛶

Copyright © Wordville

WordPress.org   WordPress on Twitter   WordPress on Facebook

THIS BOOK LEAVES SOME THINGS OUT

Big books are no fun. They're expensive to buy, heavy to carry and often written in long, complicated sentences and paragraphs and chapters that go on and on while the text grows and the words grow longer and more obscure as the author tries to show their verbosity and vocabulary, examining the thesaurus for words that describe, narrate and impress and fill up space but never quite get to the point so that the reader ends up going back to the beginning of the long confusing text and tries to re-read, but then they start wondering what's for dinner or what's on TV instead …

Yes, this book will also include some bad jokes.

This book is not intended to be a comprehensive guide to everything in WordPress. This book deliberately leaves things out. This book contains what a WordPress beginner really needs to know. You will focus on only the most important parts of WordPress so that you can understand them as easily as possible.

This book does not contain everything you could know about WordPress. It contains only what a WordPress beginner needs to know.

THIS BOOK RECOMMENDS A PROCESS

After you master the techniques in this book, you can build your own websites for companies, charities, schools, sports, or whatever else you need.

However, this book uses a specific example site and we also recommend a specific site-building process. Asking all the readers of this book to build the same site makes it easy for us to give you specific instructions, explanations, and screenshots.

It's not essential that you follow every task provided, but by following the flow of each chapter, you can get a good understanding of all the key WordPress concepts.

WordPress is incredibly flexible and provides you with many options. That is both a strength and a weakness of WordPress. To make things as clear as possible for beginners, we're going to use a specific workflow for building the Wordville website:

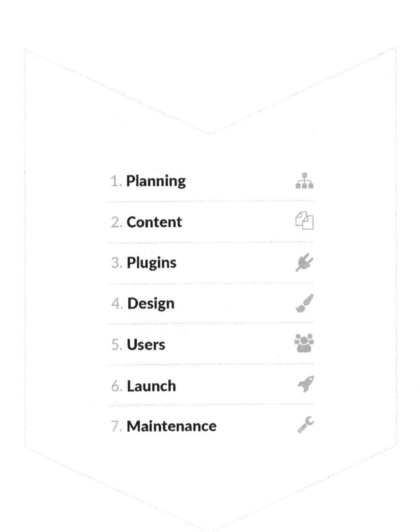

1. **Planning**

2. **Content**

3. **Plugins**

4. **Design**

5. **Users**

6. **Launch**

7. **Maintenance**

THINGS IN THIS BOOK WILL CHANGE

WordPress will change, and you must learn to adapt as it changes. We believe that everything in this book is correct at the time of writing.

However, not only does WordPress change, but so do the extra features and designs that you add on to it. As the book gets further away from its publication date, it's possible that some of the instructions and screen shots may become out of date.

One of the skills we teach you in this book is how to deal with changes in WordPress.

If you want to build modern websites, you must learn to accept and manage those changes. Please be patient with any changes you find.

Please contact me via books@ostraining.com if you find any changes. We'll update the book and send you a new copy.

WHAT DO YOU NEED FOR THIS BOOK?

Now that you know a little bit about this book, let's make sure you're ready to follow along.

You need only three things to follow along with the exercises in this book:

- A computer with an internet connection.
- A web hosting account to install WordPress.
- The resources folder downloaded
  from https://ostraining.com/books/wordpress/resources.

Yes, that's really all you need.

Before you start, you probably need to know something about WordPress. Turn to Chapter 1, and let's get started.

ABOUT THE OSTRAINING EVERYTHING CLUB

WordPress Explained is part of the OSTraining Everything Club.

The club gives you access to all of the video classes, plus all the "Explained" books from OSTraining.

- These books are always up-to-date. Because we self-publish, we can release constant updates.
- These books are active. We don't do long, boring explanations.
- You don't need any experience. The books are suitable even for complete beginners.

Join the OSTraining Everything Club today by visiting our website at https://ostraining.com. You'll be able to download ebook copies of "WordPress Explained" and all our other books and videos.

ABOUT THE OSTRAINING TEAM

Stephen Burge has split his career between teaching and web development. In 2007, he combined the two by starting to teach web development. His company, OSTraining, now teaches web design classes around the world and online. Stephen is originally from England and now lives in Florida.

This book also would not be possible without the help of the OSTraining team.

Thanks to my wife, Stacey. She has saved me from many mistakes over the years, and many terrible typos in this book.

WE OFTEN UPDATE THIS BOOK

This is version 1.6 of WordPress Explained. This version was released on March 22, 2019.

We aim to keep this book up-to-date, and so regularly release new versions to keep up with changes in WordPress.

If you find anything that is out-of-date, please email us at books@ostraining.com. We'll update the book, and to say thank you, we'll provide you with a new copy.

Many thanks to Michael Marrer of Silver Lake Wordsmiths and Harry Leeson who have already sent us feedback.

THINGS TO BE AWARE OF

We often release updates for this book. Most of the time, frequent updates are wonderful. If WordPress makes a change in the morning, we can have a new version of this book available in the afternoon. Most traditional publishers wait years and years before updating their books.

There are two disadvantages to be aware of:

- Page numbers do change. We often add and remove material from the book to reflect changes in WordPress.
- There's no index at the back of this book. This is because page numbers do change, and also because our self-publishing platform doesn't have a way to create indexes yet. We hope to find a solution for that soon.

Hopefully, you'll agree that the advantages outweigh the disadvantages. If you have any questions, we're always happy to chat: books@ostraining.com.

ARE YOU AN AUTHOR?

If you enjoy writing about the web, we'd love to talk with you.

Most publishing companies are slow, boring, inflexible and don't pay very well.

Here at OSTraining, we try to be different:

- **Fun**: We use modern publishing tools that make writing books as easy as blogging.
- **Fast**: We move quickly. Some books get written and published in less than a month.
- **Flexible**: It's easy to update your books. If technology changes in the morning, you can update your book by the afternoon.
- **Fair**: Profits from the books are shared 50/50 with the author.

Do you have a topic you'd love to write about? We publish books on almost all web-related topics.

Whether you want to write a short 100-page overview, or a comprehensive 500-page guide, we'd love to hear from you.

Contact us via email: books@ostraining.com.

ARE YOU A TEACHER?

Many schools, colleges and organizations have adopted books in our "Explained" series as a teaching guide.

This book is designed to be a step-by-step guide that students can follow at different speeds. The book can be used for a one-day class, or a longer class over multiple weeks.

If you are interested in teaching WordPress, we'd be delighted to help you with review copies, and all the advice you need.

Please email books@ostraining.com to talk with us.

Sample course outlines, descriptions, and learning outcomes are available at: https://ostraining.com/books/wordpress/classroom.

SPONSOR AN OSTRAINING BOOK

Is your company interested in sponsoring an OSTraining book?

Our books are some of the world's best-selling guides to the software they cover.

People love to read our books and learn about new web design topics.

Why not reach those people? Partner with us to showcase your company to thousands of web developers.

We have partnered with Acquia, Pantheon, Nexcess, GoDaddy, InMotion, GlowHost and Ecwid to provide sponsored training to millions of people.

If you want to learn more, visit https://marketing.ostraining.com or email us at books@ostraining.com.

WE WANT TO HEAR FROM YOU

Are you satisfied with your purchase of WordPress Explained? Let us know and help us reach others who would benefit from this book.

We encourage you to share your experience. Here are two ways you can help:

- Leave your review on Amazon's product page of WordPress Explained.
- Email your review to books@ostraining.com.

Thanks for reading WordPress Explained. We wish you the best in your future endeavors with WordPress.

THE LEGAL DETAILS

WORDPRESS EXPLAINED

Your Step-by-Step Guide to WordPress

STEPHEN BURGE

OSTraining

CONTENTS

CHAPTER 1.

WORDPRESS EXPLAINED

Before you start using WordPress, let's give you some background on WordPress itself.

By the end of this chapter, you'll know some key facts about WordPress, including:

- Who started WordPress
- Who runs WordPress
- How much WordPress costs
- Who uses WordPress

WHAT IS WORDPRESS?

WordPress is web-publishing software.

It's designed for people to publish content online: news, blogs, photos, products, documents, events or 1,001 other things.

Because it allows you to manage your content, you'll often hear it called a "Content Management System" or CMS.

WHO STARTED WORDPRESS?

It was created by Matt Mullenweg and Mike Little in 2003. Matt was a student from Texas, and Mike was a developer from England.

Both of them are still involved in WordPress today, although Matt is seen as the figurehead and makes many of the key decisions around the future of WordPress.

Matt owns a company called Automattic which runs WordPress.com and many other WordPress-related services.

WHO RUNS WORDPRESS?

WordPress is run by Matt, who is assisted by volunteers from around the world and Automattic employees.

Does this mean that a lot of work on WordPress is done for free? Yes, but that's not the whole story. Many of the volunteers also work for businesses that provide WordPress services. Companies both large and small allow their employees to spend some of their work hours on contributing to WordPress.

HOW MUCH DOES WORDPRESS COST?

Free. Yes, 100% free.

The software is free to use, free to download, free to use on your sites, free to use on your customers' sites.

There are also many free features available. You can find designs that people have created and are giving away. You can also find free shopping carts, calendars, contact forms and much more.

With all this said, there are still many companies that make a living by selling products for WordPress. If you'd like a very impressive design or feature, there are companies that sell them, typically for a price between $5 and $500.

DOES WORDPRESS HAVE A LOGO?

Yes, the WordPress logo is the letter W inside a circle. The name itself is normally spelled with an uppercase "P", so it's "WordPress".

HOW MANY VERSIONS OF WORDPRESS ARE THERE?

WordPress is always changing, and there's only ever one version of WordPress that you should be using at any given time. When a new version is released, the previous version becomes obsolete. You should always make sure you are running the latest version.

This may come as a surprise if you've used other website software before. Most web software has several different versions available at any given time.

Here's an example of how WordPress versions are released:

- WordPress 4.6: August 2016

- WordPress 4.7: December 2016

- WordPress 4.8: June 2017

- WordPress 4.9: November 2017
- WordPress 5.0: December 2018

In the future, more versions will be released, and they will be released regularly. Don't let that put you off. New versions of WordPress are like the new versions of cars. This year's Toyota, Ford or Honda might have small improvements or tweaks over last year's model, but it's instantly recognizable as the same car. You'll have little problem moving from one to the other.

The key concepts of WordPress don't change, and in this book we're going to focus on those key concepts. After you're finished, you'll hopefully be able to pick up a site using any version and be able to successfully use it.

It really is like learning to drive. You learn to drive in one type of car, but once you understand how to do it, you'll be able to quickly adapt to driving any other type of car.

WHY SHOULD YOU CHOOSE WORDPRESS?

So why should you choose WordPress instead of many other options for building a website? Here are some of the best reasons:

- **It's easier**. I can't promise that your WordPress experience will be 100% frustration-free. There will be some moments when you're stuck and wish you'd taken up knitting instead. However, WordPress is much easier than most other types of website software, and really there's not very much to learn. Once you've mastered the basics in this book, you can go out and build great WordPress sites.
- **It's quicker**. WordPress provides you with many ready-built features. If you want a new site design or to add a calendar or shopping cart to your site, you can often do it with just a few clicks. It may take a few days or even weeks to build a really

great WordPress site, but you'll be able to develop and launch more quickly than with many alternatives.

- **It's cheaper**. Building a WordPress site is unlikely to be completely cost-free because at a certain point you may need to spend some money. You may have purchased this book or other training, and you might buy a new design or feature for your site. A good WordPress site may cost you between a few dollars and thousands of dollars at the top end. However, commercial alternatives to WordPress often cost tens or hundreds of thousands of dollars.

- **It has more options**. If you'd like extra features on your WordPress site, https://wordpress.org/plugins/ is the place to go. There you can find tens of thousands of options. For example, if you'd like a calendar, there are over 400 options; and if you'd like a slideshow, there are around 500 options. All of those numbers will have probably gone up by the time you read this, so there really are a lot of choices. However, at some point you may have to hire a developer if you have very unusual or specific requirements.

WHO USES WORDPRESS?

The simple answer to this is "a lot of people"!

It's often estimated that more than one in every four websites in the world uses WordPress.

WordPress is not only used by a very large number of websites, but also by some very high-profile organizations.

Governments: Many national and regional government sites use WordPress. In the United States, the Library of Congress and the state of Wyoming both use WordPress. One particularly high-profile government site is http://sweden.se, the official website for Sweden, which is shown here:

The main website for the U.S. president also uses WordPress: http://whitehouse.gov.

Corporations: WordPress powers many business, entertainment and news websites and can handle large amounts of traffic. One great example is the shipping company UPS, whose WordPress site at http://longitudes.ups.com is shown here:

Media: Leading newspapers in many countries use WordPress. One of the most popular of these is the news site Time. Their website at http://time.com is built in WordPress, as shown here:

Education and Cultural Organizations: WordPress is particularly popular in education, with everyone from large universities to small schools using it. Many charities and non-profit organizations rely on WordPress. One of the most famous is the Canadian Museum of History, which is Canada's most-visited museum. Their website, http://www.historymuseum.ca, is shown here:

Famous People: Actors and musicians use WordPress to showcase their work for fans. One of the most famous is the Rolling Stones. Their website, http://rollingstones.com, is shown here:

WHAT'S NEXT?

In this chapter, you've learned some really important information about WordPress:

- WordPress is about 15 years old.

- WordPress is developed by volunteers who often work for WordPress companies such as Automattic.

- WordPress is 100% free to download and use.

- WordPress is always changing.

- WordPress is easier, cheaper, quicker and has more options than many of the alternative ways to build websites.

- WordPress is widely-used by media, businesses, governments and non-profit organizations.

Our next step is to dive in and start using WordPress. If you're ready, turn the page and let's begin.

CHAPTER 2.

PLANNING FOR YOUR WORDPRESS WEBSITE

You will need a WordPress website to follow along with this book.

This book is almost entirely hands-on. Throughout the remaining chapters, we're going to build a site called "Wordville". This practice website is going to be for an imaginary city where everyone loves WordPress.

Read through this chapter, and we'll give you advice on how to set up a WordPress website.

WHAT YOU NEED TO FOLLOW ALONG WITH THIS BOOK

You need only three things to follow along with this book:

1. A computer with an internet connection.
2. The folder of resources downloaded from https://ostraining.com/books/wordpress/resources/. These are images and other files you can use for the exercises in this book.
3. A blank WordPress site. I do highly recommend having a new, blank WordPress site to work with. Please don't use your company's live site when following along with this book.

So, if you don't have a blank WordPress site, where do you go to get one?

I have an easy answer! Just follow this link: http://ostraining.com/sandbox.

This will give you a blank WordPress site that you can use to follow along with this book. The site will expire 7 days after your last login, so as long as you keep learning, the site will stay alone.

If you want to export your site at the end of this book, we show you how in the chapter called, "WordPress Site Maintenance Explained".

If you want long-term hosting for your WordPress site, visit http://ostraining.com/books/wordpress/hosting.

MAKE SURE YOU'RE READY TO GO

Wonderful! You've chosen somewhere to install your WordPress website.

Go ahead and visit your new WordPress site. This will be the main URL you choose for your WordPress site.

When you visit your site, it will look similar to this next image.

Don't worry if your site doesn't look identical to that image. Some hosting companies may make some harmless changes to the default WordPress installation. If your site doesn't look like this image, visit http://ostraining.com/books/wordpress/start for instructions on how to fix that.

Sandbox — Just another WordPress site

Hello world!

Welcome to WordPress. This is your first post. Edit or delete it, then start writing!

👤 admin 🕐 January 3, 2019 📁 Uncategorized 💬 1 Comment ✏️ Edit

Search ...

Search

Recent Posts

Hello world!

- Add /wp-admin/ to your URL, so that you visit a URL like this: http://example.com/wp-admin/.

- Log in using the user details you created when installing your site.

Username or Email Address

Password

☐ Remember Me

Log In

Lost your password?

← Back to Wordville

When you log into your WordPress site, you're going to see the black, white and gray admin area that's shown below. This is the main, private dashboard for your new WordPress site. Absolutely everything you want to change about your site can be changed from here. It is the control panel of your site, where you go to add content, create navigation, or modify your site's layout.

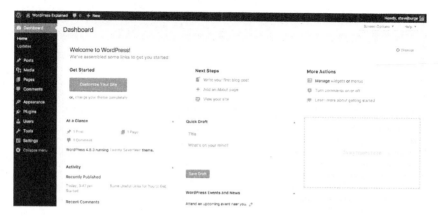

WHAT'S NEXT?

Does your WordPress test site look like the images above? Yes, then you're good to go.

Your WordPress test site still doesn't look ready? You're welcome to email us via books@ostraining.com if you have any questions about getting set up with a test site.

In the next chapter, we have some exercises to get you started with your new WordPress site.

The workflow we recommend for building WordPress websites looks like the image below. In this chapter, we've done the planning and preparation needed to get us started. Now it's time to move on to Step 2 and start creating content.

1. Planning

2. Content

3. Plugins

4. Design

5. Users

6. Launch

7. Maintenance

CHAPTER 3.

YOUR FIRST 10 WORDPRESS TASKS

In this chapter, we're going to do some warm-up exercises in your WordPress site.

The goal is not only to get you familiar with WordPress's user interface, but also to introduce you to some key WordPress features that you'll be using throughout this book.

We're not going to dive deep into any particular feature, but we will start to make some changes to your site.

We have ten small tasks that will help you feel more comfortable with WordPress:

1. Write a post
2. Format a block of text
3. Add an image
4. Add a video
5. Add a page
6. Add a comment
7. Change the theme
8. Rearrange the sidebar
9. Activate a plugin
10. Update your user account

TASK #1. WRITE A POST

Let's get started and write our first content in WordPress. The most popular option to create content in WordPress is using "Posts".

- In the black admin menu, go to "Posts" and then "Add New".

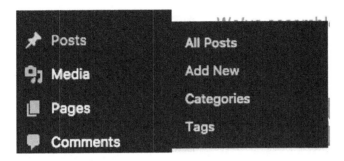

You'll see a screen like the one below. Let's start by entering a title for your post. Click your mouse in the area marked "Add title":

Start typing in this highlighted box. Here's a suggested title:

- Title: **Welcome to Wordville**

Now let's start writing the post. To write, you'll need to click in the box labelled "Start writing or type / to choose a block".

- Body: **This new website is going to talk about WordPress!**

- Go to the top-right corner of the screen and click the "Publish" button, as shown in the image below.

After clicking the "Publish" button, you'll see a sidebar asking, "Are you ready to publish? Double-check your settings before publishing."

This sidebar allows you to confirm information about your new post. For example, will it be visible to the public? Will it be published immediately? We'll learn how to configure these settings later, but for now the default choices will work perfectly.

- Click the "Publish" button again.

You'll now see at least a couple of success messages. On the left, you'll see "Post published." On the right, you'll see "Welcome to Wordville is now live."

- Click the "View Post" button:

- You'll now see your post published on your website. Your screen should look similar to the one below.

Congratulations! You've published your first WordPress blog post!

Wordville — Just another WordPress site

Welcome to Wordville

👤 stevejburge   🕐 January 15, 2019   📖 Leave a comment   ✏ Edit

This new website is going to talk about WordPress!

TASK #2. FORMAT SOME TEXT

At the moment, our first blog post is online, but it only has a single sentence of text. Let's improve our text and add some formatting.

- Click the "Edit Post" button, as shown below.

Let's add some more text. Here's the text we're going to write:

"WordPress started in 2003 with a single bit of code to enhance the typography of everyday writing and with fewer users than you can count on your fingers and toes. Since then it has grown to be the largest self-hosted blogging tool in the world, used on millions of sites and seen by tens of millions of people every day."

I also have this available online for you. In another tab, or another browser, visit https://www.ostraining.com/books/ wordpress/about/. You'll see a paragraph of text under "First Text Sample". Select and copy the text on that page.

- Either write or paste this text into your WordPress post, below the first sentence that you wrote earlier. Here's how your screen should look now:

At the moment, this text has no formatting. Let's see how to change that.

If you hover over the box with your new text, you'll see some formatting controls:

WordPress started in 2003 with a single bit of code to enhance the typography of everyday writing and with fewer users than you can count on your fingers and toes. Since then it has grown to be the largest self-hosted blogging tool in the world, used on millions of sites and seen by tens of millions of people every day.

Let's see an example of how it works.

- Select part of the text with your mouse.
- Click the "B" button.

Here's how your text will look after you've added the bold formatting:

Welcome to Wordville

This new website is going to talk about WordPress!

WordPress started in 2003 with a single bit of code to enhance the typography of everyday writing and with fewer users than you can count on your fingers and toes. Since then it has grown to the largest self-hosted blogging tool in the world, used on **millions of sites** and seen by tens of millions of people every day.

Go ahead and try that with Italic text, using the image below as a guide.

- Select part of the text with your mouse.
- Click the "I" button.

Welcome to Wordville

This new website is going to talk about WordPress!

WordPress started in 2003 with a single bit of code to enhance the typography of everyday writing and with fewer users than you can count on your fingers and toes. Since then it has grown to be the largest self-hosted blogging tool in the world, used on **millions of sites** and seen by tens of millions of people every day.

In addition to formatting, you can add headings to your text.

- In the top-left corner of your screen, click the + icon shown below:

Clicking this + icon will give you a wide range of choices. We're going to dig into these choices throughout this book.

- Click "Heading".

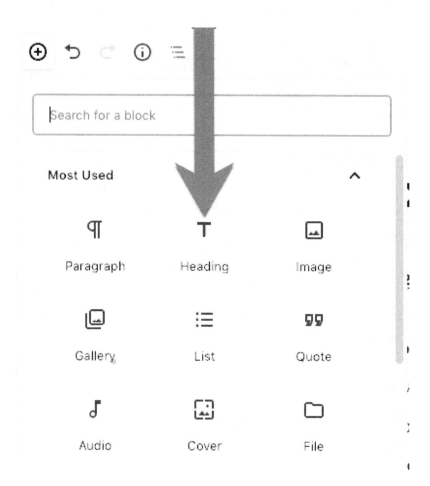

- You'll now see a new box with the label, "Write heading…".

Welcome to Wordville

This new website is going to talk about WordPress!

WordPress started in 2003 with a single bit of code to enhance the typography of everyday writing and with fewer users than you can count on your fingers and toes. Since then it has grown to be the largest self-hosted blogging tool in the world, used on **millions of sites** and seen by tens of millions of people every day.

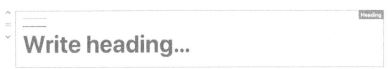

Write heading...

- In this "Write heading ..." box, let's change the text. Write "About WordPress.org".

About WordPress.org

Start writing or type / to choose a block

Now let's add some more text. I've included the text below. It's also available at https://www.ostraining.com/books/wordpress/about/ under "Second Text Sample".

"On WordPress.org, you can download and install a software script called WordPress. To do this you need a web host who meets the minimum requirements and a little time. WordPress is completely customizable and can be used for almost anything. There is also a service called WordPress.com which lets you get started with a new and free WordPress-based blog in seconds, but varies in several ways and is less flexible than the WordPress you download and install yourself."

Here's how that text will appear when you add it below your heading:

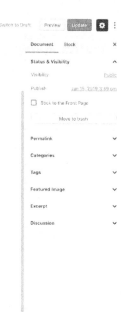

This new website is going to talk about WordPress!

WordPress started in 2003 with a single bit of code to enhance the typography of everyday writing and with fewer users than you can count on your fingers and toes. Since then it has grown to be the largest self-hosted blogging tool in the world, used on **millions of sites** and seen by tens of millions of people every day.

About WordPress.org

On WordPress.org, you can download and install a software script called WordPress. To do this you need a web host who meets the minimum requirements and a little time. WordPress is completely customizable and can be used for almost anything. There is also a service called WordPress.com which lets you get started with a new and free WordPress-based blog in seconds, but varies in several ways and is less flexible than the WordPress you download and install yourself.

There are other formatting options you can try. For example, WordPress text is aligned to the left by default, but you can align it to the center or right.

- Select all the text and click the "Align text center" button:

On WordPress.org, you can download and install a software script called WordPress. To do this you need a web host who meets the minimum requirements and a little time. WordPress is completely customizable and can be used for almost anything. There is also a service called WordPress.com which lets you get started with a new and free WordPress-based blog in seconds, but varies in several ways and is less flexible than the WordPress you download and install yourself.

This image below shows the result after you have centered the text:

About WordPress.org

On WordPress.org, you can download and install a software script called WordPress. To do this you need a web host who meets the minimum requirements and a little time. WordPress is completely customizable and can be used for almost anything. There is also a service called WordPress.com which lets you get started with a new and free WordPress-based blog in seconds, but varies in several ways and is less flexible than the WordPress you download and install yourself.

- Undo the centered alignment by selecting all the text and clicking the "Align text left" button.
- You can add links to other websites. Select the "WordPress.com" text, and then click the "Link" icon.

- Then you can enter the URL for the site you want to link to, and be sure to click the arrow to complete the process.

About WordPress.org

On WordPress.org, you can download and install a software script called WordPress. To do this you need a web host who meets the minimum requirements and a little time. WordPress is completely customizable and can be used for almost anything. There is also a service called WordPress.com which lets you get started with a new and

`http://wordpress.com` ↵ ⋮ but varies in several ways and is less flexible than the WordPress you download and install yourself.

When you've added a link, the text should be marked in blue with a line underneath:

About WordPress.org

On WordPress.org, you can download and install a software script called WordPress. To do this you need a web host who meets the minimum requirements and a little time. WordPress is completely customizable and can be used for almost anything. There is also a service called WordPress.com which lets you get started with a new and free WordPress-based blog in seconds, but varies in several ways and is less flexible than the WordPress you download and install yourself.

After you've finished experimenting with the formatting toolbar, go to the right of your screen and click "Update".

This new website is going to talk about WordPress!

WordPress started in 2003 with a single bit of code to enhance the typography of everyday writing and with fewer users than you can count on your fingers and toes. Since then it has grown to be the largest self-hosted blogging tool in the world, used on **millions of sites** and seen by tens of millions of people every day.

- Click the "Preview" button which is directly next to the "Update" button. You'll now see that your post has a lot more text, and also has some formatting, as in the screenshot below.

Wordville — Just another WordPress site

Welcome to Wordville

👤 stevejburge   🕑 January 15, 2019   📓 Leave a comment   ✏ Edit

This new website is going to talk about WordPress!

WordPress started in 2003 with a single bit of code to enhance the typography of everyday writing and with fewer users than you can count on your fingers and toes. Since then it has grown to be the largest self-hosted blogging tool in the world, used on **millions of sites** and seen by tens of millions of people every day.

About WordPress.org

TASK #3. ADD AN IMAGE

Now that you know how to format text in WordPress, let's liven up our content with images and videos.

- Keep your post editing screen open. In another tab or browser, go to https://wordpress.org/about/logos/.
- Click the "PNG (BaseGray/transparent)" link, shown in the image below.
- You'll see a copy of the WordPress logo. Download this to your desktop. The file will have the name WordPress-logotype-standard.png.

Graphics & Logos

Official WordPress Logo

When you need the official WordPress logo for a web site or publication, please use one of the following. Please only use logos in accordance with the WordPress trademark policy.

Downloads

Now let's add the WordPress logo to our post:

- Go back to your "Welcome to Wordville" post.
- Click the + icon in the top-left corner.
- Click the "Image" block.

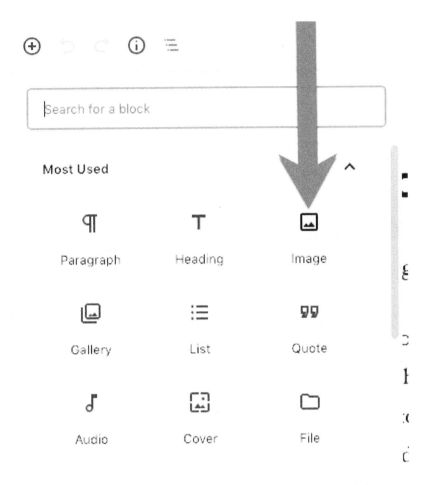

- You will now see your new Image block below the existing content.

- You can drag-and-drop the WordPress-logotype-standard.png file directly into this block area. Or you can click "Upload" and select the file from your desktop. No matter which option you choose, you'll see the WordPress logo inside your post:

Write caption ..

TASK #4. ADD A VIDEO

If anything, it's even easier to add video to WordPress posts. If the video is hosted on YouTube.com, Vimeo.com or another popular video site, then all you need to know is the URL of the video.

In this example, I've taken the URL from a video of Matt Mullenweg, one of the co-founders of WordPress. The URL is: https://www.youtube.com/watch?v=Nl6U7UotA-M. (Please note the character after "N" and before "6" in this URL is a lowercase "L" and not the number "1".)

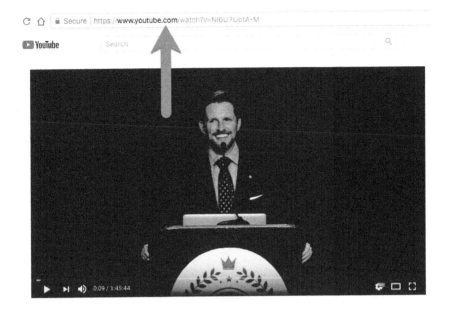

- Once you have the URL for the video, click the + icon to add a new block to your post.

- There's a search box inside the block selection popup. Search for "YouTube".

- Click "YouTube" when you've found the correct block.

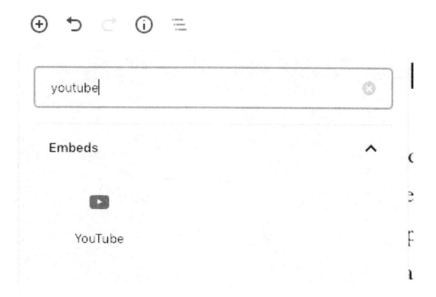

- You'll now see a YouTube block below your existing content.

- Enter the URL of the YouTube video: https://www.youtube.com/watch?v=Nl6U7UotA-M.
- Click the "Embed" button.
- WordPress will automatically turn the link into a video:

Write caption...

Now that you've added these changes, let's see how your post looks with an image and video.

- Click the "Update" button to save your changes.

- Click the "Preview" button and you'll see your post now looks much more interesting!

TASK #5. ADD A PAGE

To start this next task, you need to return to the WordPress dashboard.

- Go to the top of the screen and hover over your site name.

- Click the "Dashboard" link that appears under your site name.

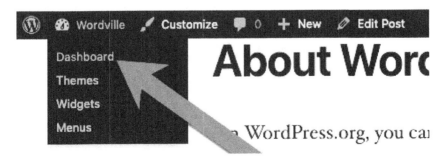

In this task, we're going to add more content.

This time, we're using the "Pages" option, rather than "Posts". What's the difference between Posts and Pages? Let's create a Page and see what differences we can see.

- Go to "Pages" and then "Add New".

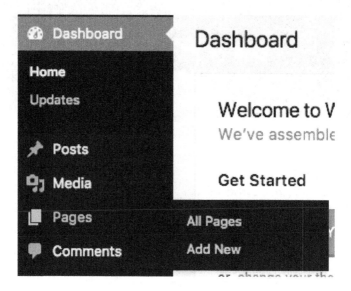

Enter the following details:

- Title: **About Wordville**
- Body: **Wordville is a fun city where everyone loves WordPress.**

About Wordville

Wordville is a fun city where everyone loves WordPress.

- Click the "Publish" button twice.

- Click the "View page" link at top of the screen or the "View page" button in the right sidebar.
- You'll now see that your page is visible on the site:

About Wordville

Wordville is a fun city where everyone loves WordPress.

Edit

So Pages are similar to Posts, but have several small differences. What exactly are those differences?

These are some of the differences you might notice:

- Posts show the date they were published. This is because they contain time-sensitive content. Pages don't show the date they were published. The reason for this is because their content is timeless.
- Posts often have URLs containing the date they were published. For example, http://wpexplained.com/2019/1/20/welcome-to-wordville/. Pages have short, simple URLs with no date. For example, http://wpexplained.com/about-wordville/.
- Posts show the name of the author. Pages don't show the name of the author.
- Posts have an area for comments underneath the body. Pages don't have a comments area.

- Posts appear on your site's homepage automatically. Pages don't appear on your site's homepage.

Why do Posts and Pages have these different features?

- Posts are for timely, topical and opinionated content. For topical content, the date is important. For opinionated content, the author name and date are important.

- Pages are for static content that rarely changes. Good examples of Pages include your "About Us", "Terms and Conditions", and "Location" pages. None of the content on those pages is likely to change very often. Also, the name of the author isn't important, and you probably don't want people to leave comments.

TASK #6. ADD A COMMENT

In the previous task, we noticed that Posts have comments, but Pages do not.

But, what does it mean to leave a comment in WordPress? Let's find out.

- In your WordPress dashboard, click "Posts".
- Click "View" under the "Welcome to Wordville" link:

- Scroll down to the bottom of your post and find the "Comment" area. It will look like this next image.

- Leave a comment and click "Post Comment".

Leave a comment

Comment

- Your comment will instantly be published:

Join the Conversation

🗩 1 Comment

 **stevejburge**
February 3, 2019 at 1:46 pm — ✎ Edit

WordPress seems really exciting.

Thanks for this info!

Reply

- Go back to your WordPress dashboard. As we saw earlier, often the quickest way to do this is via the "Dashboard" link in your admin menu.
- Click the "Comments" link on the left side of the site. You'll now be able to see all the comments on your Posts.

On this screen, you can manage your comments. If you don't want a particular comment on your site, you can click "Unapprove", "Spam", or "Trash". If you like the comment, you can also click "Reply" and continue the discussion right here.

TASK #7. CHANGE THE THEME

You've been kind enough not to email me yet and ask the following question:

Steve, why does our site look so boring and white?

(Only joking, you're welcome to get in touch: books@ostraining.com)

If you had been thinking this, then you're right. The site looks very plain. In this task, let's change the theme to something that is more exciting to look at.

- Go to "Appearance" and then "Themes".

You'll now see at least three themes to choose from. WordPress releases a new theme almost every year, so these themes are named after the year they were released.

- We're going to choose the "Twenty Seventeen" theme. Click the "Activate" button.

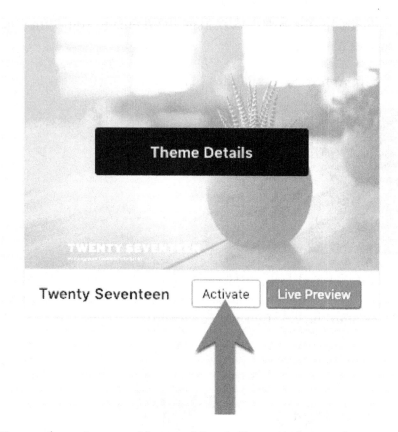

Now we're going to add some Wordville-specific touches to our new theme.

- Click the blue "Customize" button for Twenty Seventeen:

You'll now see a full-screen page designer for your WordPress site:

- On the left-hand side are lots of configuration options.
- If you click on any of the blue pencil icons, you'll automatically be taken to the relevant configuration option.

- Click on the blue pencil next to "WORDVILLE", as shown in the next image. Your site title may be different, but we're going to fix that now.

You can now edit your "Site Title" and "Tagline" settings:

- Site Title: **Wordville**
- Tagline: **A city that loves WordPress**

While we're here, we can also upload a logo for our site.

- Click the "Select logo" button.
- Upload the file called wordville-logo.png from the Resources

folder. If you haven't download this yet, go to https://ostraining.com/books/wordpress/resources/. These are images and other files you can use for the exercises in this book.

• After uploading the logo, you'll see a "Crop Image" screen. Later in the book we'll explain more about image cropping and editing, but for this task you can click the "Crop Image" button. It won't make any changes to your image.

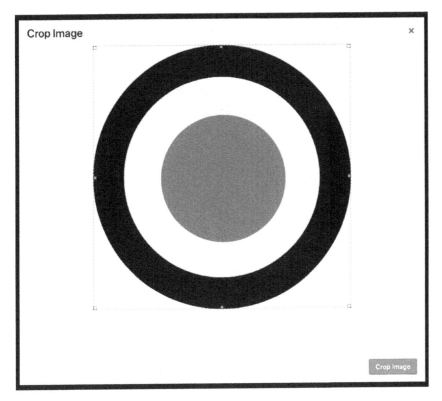

• Now you will see your new image is visible in the "Logo" area:

Logo

Remove   Change logo

Site Title

Wordville

Let's repeat that process for the "Site Icon" option. This is down in the bottom-left corner of the sidebar.

As WordPress explains, Site Icons are what you see in browser tabs, bookmark bars. They are also often called "favicons".

- Click "Select image" for the Site Icon:

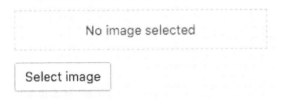

- Browse through the images you have uploaded to your site.
- Select the same wordville-logo.png image that you used for the Logo.
- You will now see this image used for your Site Icon also:

Next, let's change the header image for our site.

- To do this we will need to exit the "Site Identity" area. Click the arrow next to "Site Identity".

- Click "Header Media" in the left column, as shown in the image below.

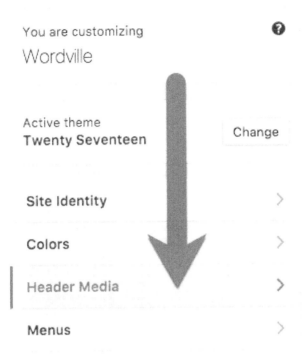

You are customizing ❓

Wordville

Active theme
Twenty Seventeen   Change

Site Identity   >

Colors   >

Header Media   >

Menus   >

- Click "Add new image", as shown here.

Header Image

Click "Add new image" to upload an image file from your computer. Your theme works best with an image that matches the size of your video — you'll be able to crop your image once you upload it for a perfect fit.

Current header

| Hide image | Add new image |

- Open the "Wordville Resources" folder that you downloaded.
- Upload the file wordville-header.jpg.
- Click the blue "Select and Crop" button in the bottom-right corner.
- WordPress will suggest that you crop your image. Click the blue "Crop Image" button.

- You'll now see you have a new header image for your site!

- To complete the change, click the blue "Publish" button in the top-left corner.

- To exit this screen, you can click the X, next to the "Publish" button:

- Click the "Wordville" link in the top-left corner.

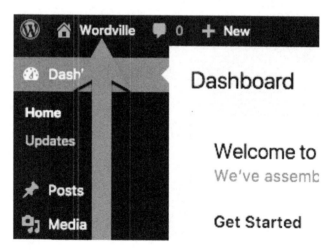

- You can now see the Site Icon live in your browser tab:

- You can also see the new, large header image in action on your site:

TASK #8. REARRANGE THE SIDEBAR

Looking at your site, you can see your header and your content. However, there's a sidebar with several small boxes. These are called "widgets". You can see:

- A Search box
- A list of Recent Posts

- A list of Recent Comments
- A link to Archives, or posts organized by the month of publication
- A list of Categories that can be used to organize posts
- A box called "Meta" with several useful links

Search ...   🔍

RECENT POSTS

Welcome to Wordville

RECENT COMMENTS

stevejburge on Welcome to Wordville

ARCHIVES

November 2017

CATEGORIES

Uncategorized

META

Site Admin

Log out

You can organize and control these widgets. Here's how it's done:

- Click the "Customize" link in your admin menu, as shown here.

- Click the pencil icon next to any of the widgets in the sidebar:

In the left sidebar, you can now configure these widgets.

- Enter "Search Wordville" in the "Title" area for the Search widget.

- You'll see this reflected immediately in the main part of the screen, as shown in the image below.

You can also rearrange and remove widgets in here:

- Try dragging-and-dropping these widgets to change the order.

- Try clicking "Remove" for the "Meta" widget:

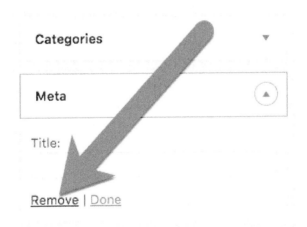

- After making those changes, your list of widgets might look like this:

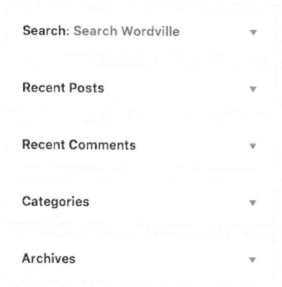

Search: Search Wordville ▼

Recent Posts ▼

Recent Comments ▼

Categories ▼

Archives ▼

Visit the front of your site, and you'll see that your design has been transformed since the start of the chapter. You have new content, a new header image, and a new logo!

TASK #9. ACTIVATE A PLUGIN

In the previous few tasks, we changed how your site looks.

This task is not going to bring such major changes, but it will show you how to add new features for your WordPress site.

- Go to the "Plugins" link in your site's dashboard:

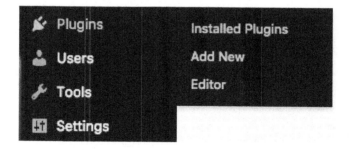

You'll see two plugins. These both offer extra features for your WordPress site.

- Akismet: This plugin can protect your blog from spam. We show you how to use Akismet in the chapter, "WordPress Site Maintenance Explained".
- Hello Dolly: This shows lyrics from the "Hello Dolly" musical inside your site.

You think I'm joking about that last plugin? Trust me, I'm not!

- Click the "Activate" button next to "Hello Dolly".

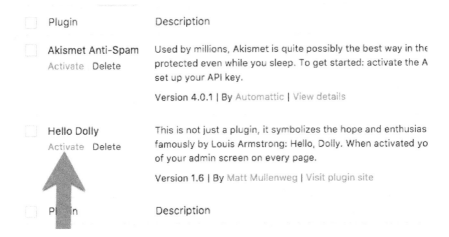

	Plugin	Description
	Akismet Anti-Spam Activate Delete	Used by millions, Akismet is quite possibly the best way in the protected even while you sleep. To get started: activate the A set up your API key. Version 4.0.1 | By Automattic | View details
	Hello Dolly Activate Delete	This is not just a plugin, it symbolizes the hope and enthusias famously by Louis Armstrong: Hello, Dolly. When activated yo of your admin screen on every page. Version 1.6 | By Matt Mullenweg | Visit plugin site
	Pl n	Description

Look up in the top-right corner of your site. Every time you load a new page, you'll now see a quote from "Hello Dolly".

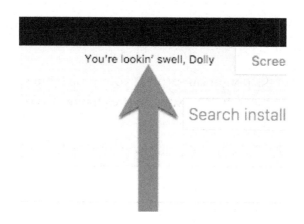

If you're a little confused about what Hello Dolly is, allow me to suggest some background reading! https://en.wikipedia.org/wiki/Hello,_Dolly!_(musical)

Why is this plugin inside WordPress? Partly it's there as joke, and to offer a touch of humor. Partly it's there as an example, for tutorials like this. Partly it's there because of tradition – it's been in WordPress for 15 years now.

TASK #10. UPDATE YOUR USER ACCOUNT

For our final task, let's update your user profile.

- In the top-right corner, use the pull-down menu and click "Edit My Profile".

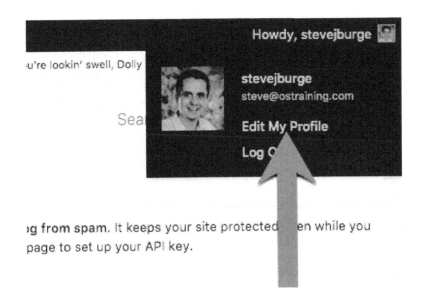

ıu're lookin' swell, Dolly

ıg from spam. It keeps your site protected en while you
page to set up your API key.

- On this next screen, you can choose your personal settings for this site. For example, you can change the color of the admin dashboard. "Ectoplasm" offers a purple color scheme. We're going to use the black color scheme throughout this book, but it won't hurt if you choose a different color.

- You can also control how your name is displayed throughout the site. Until now, my name has been showing as "stevejburge". I can fix that using the setting called "Display name publicly as":

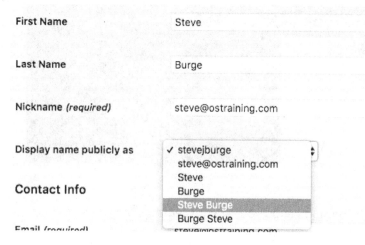

First Name	Steve
Last Name	Burge
Nickname *(required)*	steve@ostraining.com

Display name publicly as

✓ stevejburge
steve@ostraining.com
Steve
Burge
Steve Burge
Burge Steve

Contact Info

Fmail *(required)*

- If you're wondering why my photo is being used by WordPress, that's because I've registered on a site called Gravatar.com. If you'd like to change your profile photo, but don't have an account on http://gravatar.com yet, you can follow these instructions: http://ostraining.com/blog/wordpress/gravatar.

Profile Picture

You can change your profile picture on Gravatar.

WHAT'S NEXT?

Congratulations. You've just completed ten tasks that have you thinking about WordPress. You've already mastered several important site features, and you've made major changes to your site's design.

In the next chapter, we're going to dig deeper into posts. Your WordPress site is all about content, and posts are the most important content on most WordPress sites.

At the end of this chapter, your site should look like the image below. Don't worry if it's not an exact match. So long as you feel comfortable with the ten tasks in this chapter, you're ready to move on.

CHAPTER 4.

WORDPRESS POSTS EXPLAINED

In this chapter, we are going to take a look at posts in WordPress. WordPress started out as a blogging platform, and as a result it's really excellent at blogging. A blog is basically an online journal or diary. Posts are entries in that journal or diary. But they don't have to be, there are lots of different things that have dated content like that.

We are building a site for Wordville, and so we are going to use posts as news items. If you think about it, they are very similar. News items have a headline, some content and a date, which is exactly like a blog post or journal entry.

After completing this chapter, you should be able to:

- Use more advanced features in the text editor.
- Use the publishing features for WordPress posts.
- Choose which Screen Options you want to show.
- Manage content directly from the All Posts screen.
- Put together everything you've learned so far and create a media rich post.

CREATING MORE POSTS

On your main WordPress dashboard, there may be as many as three different ways to create a new post:

- From the left hand menu, there is the "Posts" button.
- At the admin bar at the very top of the page, there is a "+ New" button, which allows you to add a new post. ✗ Best
- On the dashboard itself, there's a "Write your first blog post" link.

All three of these do the exact same thing, so it doesn't matter which one you click. The one in the admin bar is always with you as long as you are logged in, so it may become the most useful.

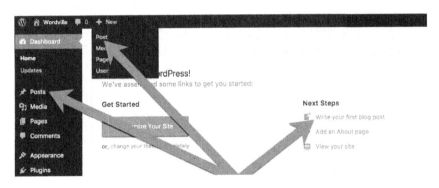

The image below shows the "Add New Post" page.

Let's add a second blog post to our WordPress site.

- Title: **Join the Annual WordPress Events!**
- Body: **Every year WordPress holds a major event in Europe and North America. In 2018, thousands of WordPress fans met in Nashville and Belgrade.**

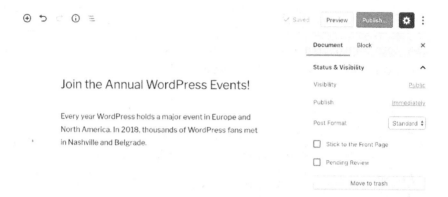

You create WordPress posts using blocks. Almost everything you want to add to WordPress is available as a block. Let's see some examples in this chapter. First, let's add a list of recent WordPress events.

- Click the + icon in the top-left corner.
- Choose the "List" block.

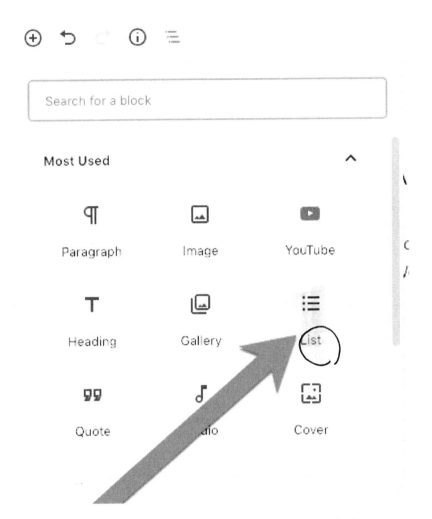

You'll now see a new block with bullet points ready for you to use:

Join the Annual WordPress Events!

Every year WordPress holds a major event in Europe and North America. In 2018,

 and Belgrade.

Enter the following bullets:

- 2017: Nashville and Paris
- 2016: Philadelphia and Vienna
- 2015: Philadelpha and Seville

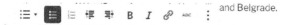 and Belgrade.

- 2017| Nashville and Paris
- 2016: Philadelphia and Vienna
- 2015: Philadelpha and Seville

Let's explore another block. This time we'll add a "Quote" block.

- Click the + icon in the top-left corner.
- Choose the "Quote" block.

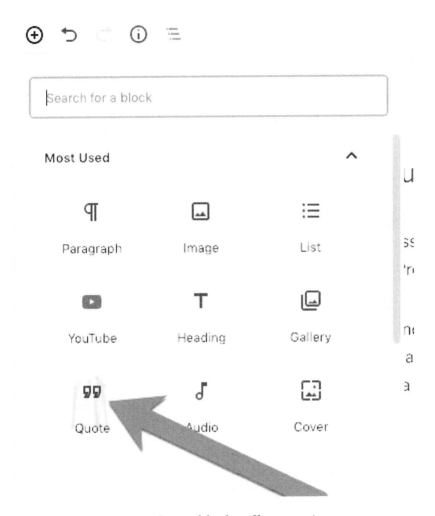

Here is how the empty Quote block will appear in your post:

Write citation...

- Type: **I went to WordCamp US in Nashville in 2018. It was great! You should come and join us in 2019!**

- Citation: Steve from OSTraining

::: I went to WordCamp US in Nashville in 2018. It was great! You should come and join us in 2019!

Steve from OSTraining

REORDERING WORDPRESS BLOCKS

WordPress blocks are organized vertically on the page, but they can be rerranged. Let's see how to reorder our blocks.

- Click the + icon in the top-left corner.
- Choose the "Heading" block.

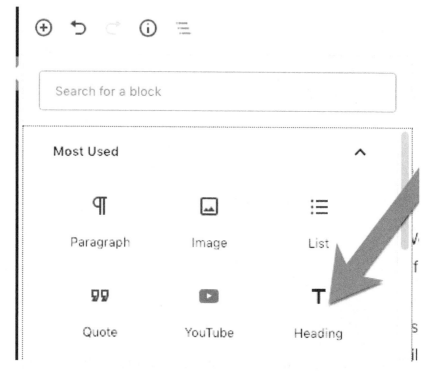

- Heading: **Recent WordPress Events**

::: Recent WordPress Events

By default, WordPress blocks are added to to the bottom of the screen. However, this heading should be placed above the List block we created earlier.

- Select the up arrow next to the "Recent WordPress Events" block.

- 2017: Nashville and Paris
- 2016: Philadelphia and Vienna
- 2015: Philadelpha and Seville

I went to WordCamp US in Nashville in 2018. It was great! You should come and join us in 2019!

::: Recent WordPress Events

- Click the up arrow twice so that your new Heading block appears above the List block:

Join the Annual WordPress Events!

Every year WordPress holds a major event in Europe and North America. In 2018, thousands of WordPress fans met in Nashville and Belgrade.

Recent WordPress Events

- 2017: Nashville and Paris
- 2016: Philadelphia and Vienna
- 2015: Philadelpha and Seville

Let's try another approach to reordering our blocks.

- Click the + icon in the top-left corner.
- Choose the "Heading" block.
- Heading: **A Happy WordPress Event Attendee**
- Select the box with six dots. It's just underneath the up arrow we used in the previous step:

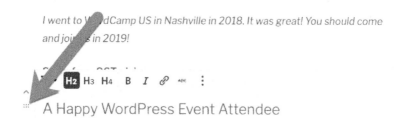

You can now drag-and-drop this block to a new place on the screen. This process can be a little tricky, but you'll get it with practice. Try to place this Heading block above the Quote block.

Recent WordPress Events

- 2017: Nashville and Paris
- 2016: Philadelphia and Vienna
- 2015: Philadelpha and Seville

I went to WordCamp US in Nashville in 2018. It was great! You should come and join us in 2019!

Steve from OSTraining

USING THE OLD WORDPRESS EDITOR

In previous versions of WordPress, there was a different editing experience. Before 2019, there were no blocks. All you saw was a single screen with all the features compressed into a single editing toolbar. If you are an old WordPress user, or want that unified experience, I'm going to show you how to get the experience back again.

- Click the + icon in the top-left corner.
- Choose the "Classic" block. This will produce a block that has two lines of editing options.

A Happy WordPress Event Attendee

I went to WordCamp US in Nashville in 2018. It was great! You should come and join us in 2019!

Steve from OS Training

Many of these features have now been moved into blocks For example, there are list icons here. Those are now available as List blocks.

There is also a "Read more" option. That is the third icon from the right in the top row. However, that is now available as a "More" block:

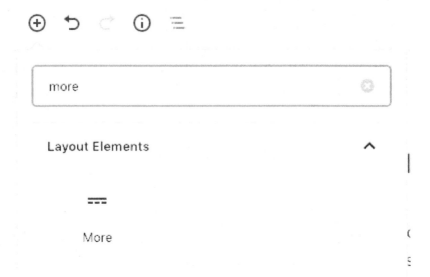

If you have used WordPress before, you may find the "Classic" block useful. However, I recommend that you take advantage of the individual blocks such as Heading, List, Quote, and Image. You will find it easier to create and organize your WordPress content if you use blocks for everything.

USING THE BLOCK TOOLBAR

Each WordPress block has a small toolbar that's availably directly over the block. This image shows the toolbar over the Paragraph block.

¶ ▾ ≡ ≡ ≡ B *I* & ᴬᴮᶜ ⋮

Every year WordPress holds a major event in Europe and North America. In 2018, thousands of WordPress fans met in Nashville and Belgrade.

The icon on the left allows you to change the block type. This only works for similar blocks: you can't change a YouTube block to a Quote block. We are looking at a Paragraph block, so this "Change block type" icon allows us to choose a Heading, List,

Quote, Preformatted or Verse blocks. Those options are available because they are also text blocks.

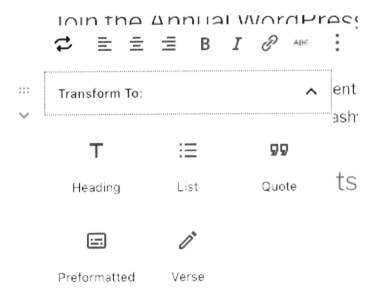

Elsewhere on the toolbar are some formatting options. From left-to-right you can see these options:

- Align text left
- Align text center
- Align text right
- Bold
- Italic
- Link
- Strikethrough

Let's take a look at the Link feature, which is one of the most important options in the toolbar.

... .- ....>> LVCI ILS!

¶ ▾ ≣ ≣ ≣ **B** *I* 🔗 ᴬᴮᶜ ⋮

Every year WordPress hold... ...ior event in Europe and North America. In 2018, thousands of WordPress fan... ...et in Nashville and Belgrade.

- Add a new sentence to this Paragraph block: **Click here to see all the WordPress events.**
- Using your cursor, select your new text.
- Click the Link icon.

Join the Annual WordPress Events!

¶ ▾ ≣ ≣ ≣ **B** *I* 🔗 ᴬᴮᶜ ⋮

Every year WordPress holds a major event in Europe and North America. In 2018, thousands of WordPress fans met in Nashville and Belgrade. Click here to see all the WordPress events.

- Enter this URL: https://central.wordcamp.org/
- Click the arrow marked below. This will add the link to the text.

Join the Annual WordPress Events!

¶ ▾ ≣ ≣ ≣ **B** *I* 🔗 ᴬᴮᶜ ⋮

Every year WordPress holds a major event in Europe and No... ...h America. In 2018, thousands of WordPress fans met in Nashville and Belgrad... ...lick here to see all the WordPress events.

https://central.wordcamp.org/   ↵ ⋮

- You'll now have a new link added to your Paragraph block:

Join the Annual WordPress Events!

Every year WordPress holds a major event in Europe and North America. In 2018, thousands of WordPress fans met in Nashville and Belgrade. Click here to see all the WordPress events.

Finally, look for the three dots in the top-right corner of the block. This icon hides several important block options. For example, you can use these options to duplicate your block. You can also insert another block directly before or after this block. That saves the hassle of creating a block at the bottom of the screen and then moving it up.

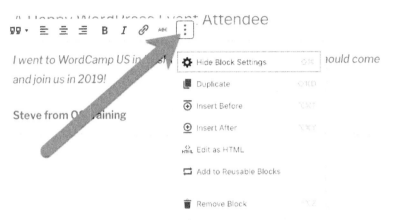

Notice the "Add to Resuable Blocks" link in the image above? This is a really useful feature.

- Click the "Add to Resuable Blocks" link for a block.
- Enter a name for the block.
- Click "Save".

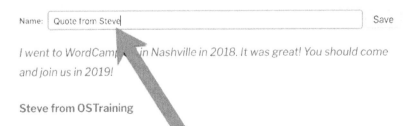

Now when you add a new block, there will be a "Reusable" area of the screen. You can easily access any block that you have saved.

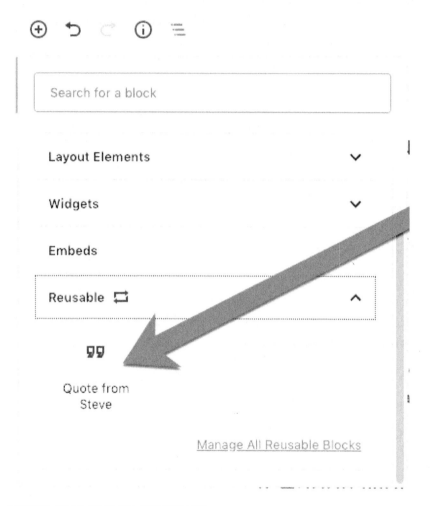

USING THE BLOCK SETTINGS

Every block has a toolbar, and it also has settings in the right sidebar. For example, place your cursor into the first Paragraph block. In the right sidebar, you'll see configuration options. In this example, you can change the Font Size, Background Color and Text Color for this block. You can also add a Drop Cap, which means the first letter will appear to be over-sized.

The Paragraph block has more features than most. Some blocks only have a couple of options, as is the case with the Heading block, shown below.

EXTRA POST FEATURES

In the top-left corner of WordPress posts, you'll find several useful tools. Next to the + icon, you can see "Undo" and "Redo" buttons. WordPress remembers all your changes, so you can use these buttons to undo or redo any changes to your post.

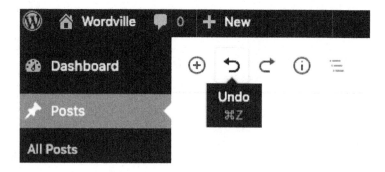

Next to the Undo and Redo buttons, you'll find a "Content structure" icon. This gives you an overview of your post. You'll see the number of words, headings, paragraphs and blocks.

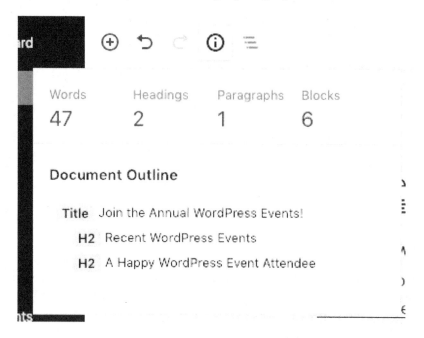

The fifth icon up here is called "Block navigation" and it will give you a clear overview of the blocks in this post. Click on any of these links and WordPress will automatically take you to that block. This can be very useful if you have a long and busy post.

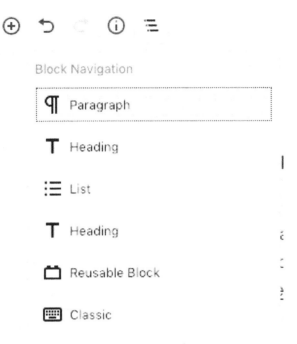

THE EXTRA PUBLISHING FEATURES INSIDE THE POST SCREEN

Look over to the right-hand side of the screen, and you'll see a series of extra features to give you more control over your content.

Make sure you have clicked the "Document" link. This box has a powerful set of publishing tools.

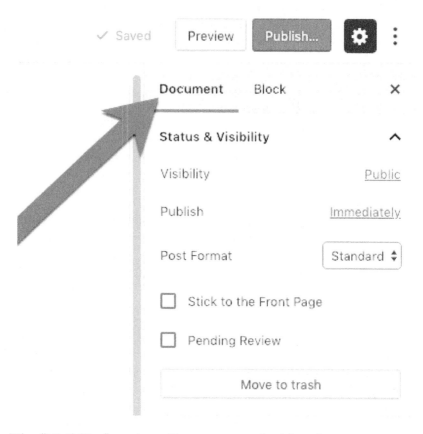

The "Visibility" option allows you to decide who can see your content. The default is "Public", but you can choose to keep this post "Private" so that only high-level users on your site can access it.

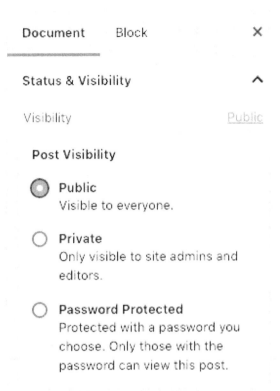

You can choose to publish your post now, or in the future. The default setting is "Immediately", but click on that link and you can choose a publishing date and time in the future.

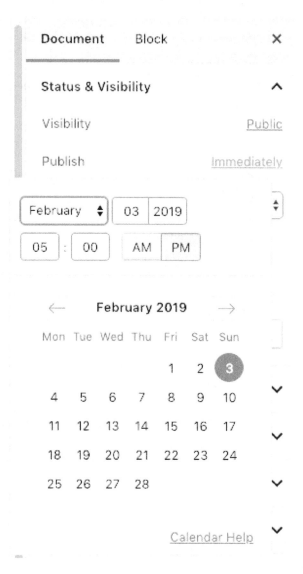

In the next image, you see that just under the "Status & Visibility" box are two more boxes. One is called "Categories" and the other is called "Tags". These are two ways to organize your content. They are important, and we'll look at them in more detail in the next chapter.

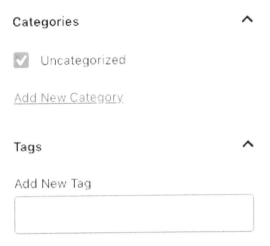

Below the "Tags" box, you see the "Featured Image" box. With the "Featured Image" option, you can associate an image with this post. Where your image appears can vary. Different themes will put the "Featured Image" in different places. For example, it might display the image at the top, side, or bottom of the post.

Let's see where our theme will place the Featured Image.

- Click "Set featured image".
- Upload the wordcamp-logos.png file from your Resources folder.

- Click the "Set featured image" button.
- You'll now see the new image appears in the box, as in the image below.

- Click the "Publish" button twice in the top-right corner of the site.
- Visit your post on the front of the site, and you'll see the header image above the post:

FEBRUARY 3, 2019 BY STEVEJBURGE

Join the Annual WordPress Events!

Recent WordPress Events

Every year WordPress holds a major event in Europe and North America. In 2018, thousands of WordPress fans met in Nashville and Belgrade. Click here to see all the WordPress events.

SEARCH WORDVILLE

Search...

RECENT POSTS

Join the Annual WordPress Events!

Welcome to Wordville

Are you clumsy?

Are any of your work colleagues sometimes a little clumsy?

If so, you'll love the Revisions features.

WordPress saves a copy of your work every time you click on the "Publish" button. Both the old and new versions will be saved. If you made a mistake, you can then roll back to an earlier version.

You can access the Revisions feature via the "Revisions" box, as shown below.

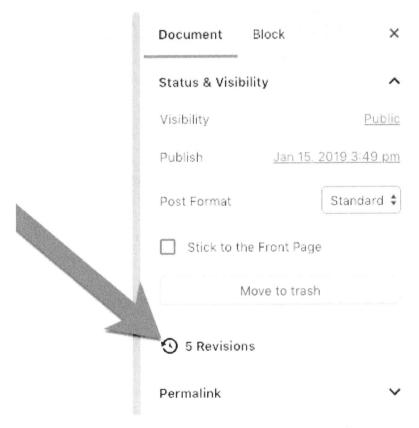

- Click the "Browse" link.

- You'll see a page like the one below with an old copy of your post in red. The current version is in green.

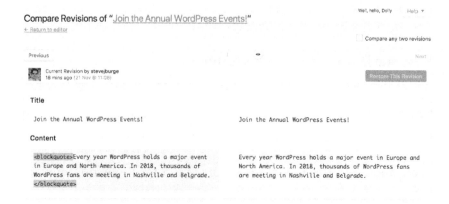

- You can use the slider bar at the top to move between different versions.

- If you want to roll back to a previous version, click the "Restore This Revision" button, as shown below.

To exit the Revisions screen, click the "Return to editor" link in the top-left corner:

So, don't worry if you make a mistake when writing your posts. You can always go back to the previous versions.

Plus, it gets better than that. WordPress saves a copy of your blog post every few seconds. So, if you your computer shuts off, you lose your internet connection, or your tab gets closed, your post will still be there and you will be able to retrieve it. You will see a message like this, offering to restore the version you lost:

EXPLORING THE "ALL POSTS" SCREEN

In this section, we are going to take a look at how your posts are organized in the admin area.

- Click the "All Posts" link in the admin menu.

Here you can see a list of your posts and a variety of information about the individual posts:

- Title
- Author
- Categories
- Tags
- Number of Comments
- Date of Publication

You can change the way these are displayed.

- Click on "Date" and you'll see the posts displayed by date.
- Click on "Title" and you'll see the posts displayed alphabetically.

You could also invert the date, so that you could see the oldest posts first instead of the most recent posts first.

- Click on either "Author", "Categories", or "Tags", and you'll see only posts that are related to that specific author, category or tag.

In the top right, there is a "Search" box. Once you have more than a dozen posts, it can be very convenient to be able to search for a specific post using keywords.

If you hover over a post, you will see a number of options: "Edit", "Quick Edit", "Trash", and "View", as shown below.

☐ Title

☐ Join the Annual WordPress Events!
Edit   Quick Edit   Trash   View

The "Quick Edit" feature is useful. It allows you to quickly modify the following important settings:

- Title
- Slug
- Date
- Password, or make the post Private
- Categories
- Tags
- Status

Also a very useful feature is the "Bulk Edit" setting. You can select many different posts and change many attributes of the posts all at once.

- Select the posts you want to bulk edit.
- Select "Edit" and "Apply".
- You'll now have the ability to edit all of these posts at the same time:

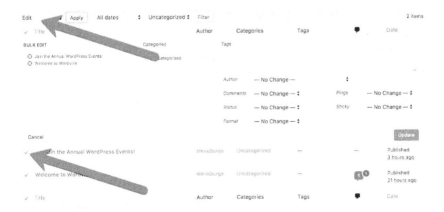

ARE YOU READY FOR A CHALLENGE?

During the last two chapters, you've learned many key skills about Posts. Now I have a challenge for you.

In the Resources folder you downloaded, there's a folder called /post-challenge/. Inside there, you'll find:

- Text for the body of your post
- An image to use as the featured image
- A logo to place inside the text

Can you create a new post that looks like the image below?

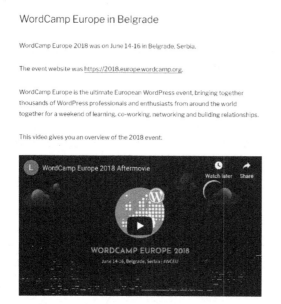

When you publish this challenge post, it should look like this image below:

FEBRUARY 3, 2019 BY STEVE BURGE

WordCamp Europe in Belgrade

Search ...

WordCamp Europe 2018 was on June 14-16 in Belgrade, Serbia.

The event website was https://2018.europe.wordcamp.org.

RECENT POSTS

WordCamp Europe is the ultimate European WordPress event, bringing together thousands of WordPress professionals and enthusiasts from around the world together for a weekend of learning, co-working, networking and building relationships.

WordCamp Europe in Belgrade

Join the Annual WordPress Events!

Welcome to Wordville

This video gives you an overview of the 2018 event:

RECENT COMMENTS

steve on Welcome to Wordville

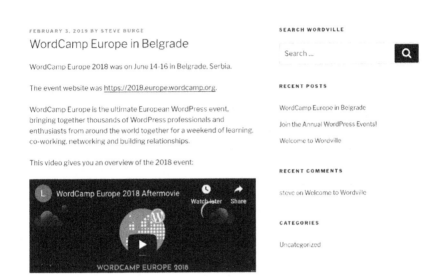

CATEGORIES

Uncategorized

WHAT'S NEXT?

In this chapter, you've explored many of the more powerful features you can use to create posts in WordPress.

As your write posts, you'll need some way to categorize them.

In the next chapter, we look at Categories and Tags and explore how you can use them to organize your content.

CHAPTER 5.

WORDPRESS CATEGORIES AND TAGS EXPLAINED

In this chapter, we are going to focus on how to organize your content.

WordPress offers two ways to organize your content: categories and tags.

These features can help you organize your content and make it easier for your readers to find the information they are looking for.

After this chapter, you'll be able to:

- Create categories, including parent categories.

- Update and manage categories.

- Understand the difference between categories and tags.

CREATING CATEGORIES

- In your WordPress site, make sure you're on the "All Posts" screen.

- Notice that all three of your posts are already in a category called "Uncategorized":

- Every post must be in at least one category. You can test this by hovering over the a post name and clicking the "Quick Edit" button

- Uncheck the "Uncategorized" box.

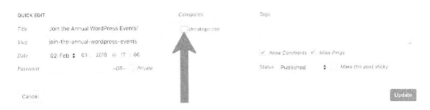

- Click "Update" and you'll see that post has returned to the "Uncategorized" category. It is impossible to remove all the categories from a post.

"Uncategorized" doesn't make much sense as a category name, so we're going to change this post from being "Uncategorized" to having a good category.

Our first posts are about events, so let's create an "Events" category.

- Open up your "WordCamp Europe in Belgrade" post.

- Open the "Categories" box in the sidebar.

- Click on the "Add New Category" link.

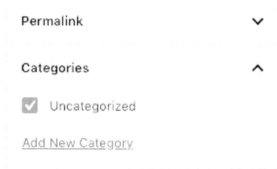

- Type in "Events".
- Click the "Add New Category" button.

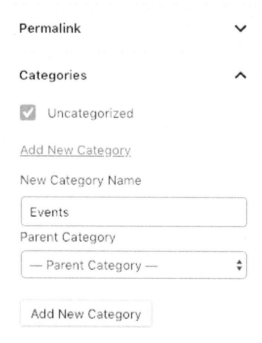

- Uncheck the "Uncategorized" button.

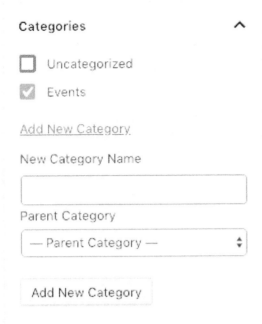

- Click "Update" at the top of the page, and the change will take effect.

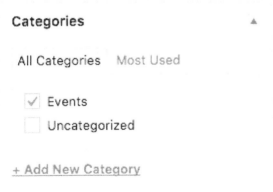

Now when you visit the front of our site, you will notice that your post says "Events", as shown in the next image. If you click on the link to "Events", you will find all posts that fall under that category. At the moment, there is only one post there.

This video gives you an overview of the 2018 event:

RECENT COMMENTS

steve on Welcome to Wordville

CATEGORIES

Events

Uncategorized

ARCHIVES

February 2019

January 2019

You can also have child categories. For example, we may want to divide our events according to location. We can add "North American Events", "European Events", "Asian Events", "African Events", and more within the "Events" category.

- Go back to edit your "WordCamp Europe in Belgrade" post.

- Add a "North American Events" category.

- Click on the "Parent Category" menu.

- Select "Events" as the "Parent" category.

- Click "Add New Category".

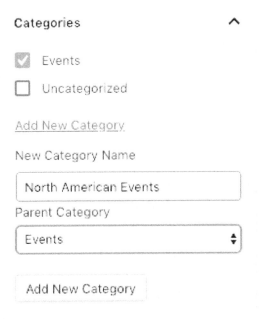

- Repeat these steps for "European Events", "Asian Events", and "African Events". As you can see, your posts can be in more than one category:

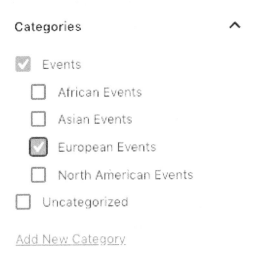

- Visit the front of your site, and you will see that your post shows all the categories you have chosen:

One question we often get asked at this point is, "How many Categories should I add to my posts?" I'd recommend reading this post to get some advice from a variety of experts: http://ostra.in/max-min-tags. However, the general conclusion is that no more than two to five categories should be used on a single post.

MANAGING CATEGORIES

You can add categories while creating posts, but this doesn't allow us full control over categories.

For example, we still have a category called "Uncategorized".

There is another way to manage categories.

- On the left hand menu under "Posts", there is a "Categories" link, as shown in the image below.

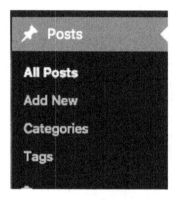

- From this view, we can create, edit, delete or view categories:

- Cick on "Edit" for the "Uncategorized" category, and you'll see the following screen:

Edit Category

Name	Uncategorized *The name is how it appears on your site.*
Slug	uncategorized *The "slug" is the URL-friendly version of the name. It is usually all lowercase and contains only letters, numbers, and hyphens.*
Parent Category	None ⬍ *Categories, unlike tags, can have a hierarchy. You might have a Jazz category, and under that have children categories for Bebop and Big Band. Totally optional.*
Description	 *The description is not prominent by default; however, some themes may show it.*

Here we can change the Name, Slug, Parent Category, and we can add a Description. The description may or may not show up on the front of the site, depending on which theme you use.

- Let's change our "Uncategorized" category to a category called "Wordville", as in the image below.
- Click "Update" when you are done.

This will now be the default category for our posts.

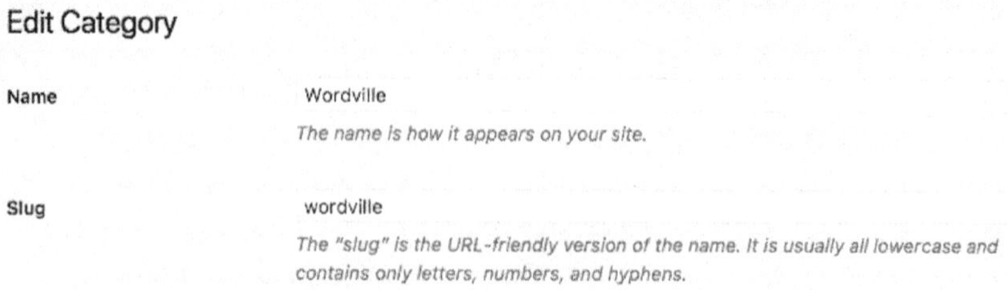

Edit Category

Name   Wordville

The name is how it appears on your site.

Slug   wordville

The "slug" is the URL-friendly version of the name. It is usually all lowercase and contains only letters, numbers, and hyphens.

On the main "Categories" screen, you can quickly add more categories. Let's take you through a quick example:

- Go to "Add New Category".
- Name: **WordPress News**
- Click "Add New Category".

Add New Category

Name

| WordPress News |

The name is how it appears on your site.

Slug

The "slug" is the URL-friendly version of the name. It is usually all lowercase and contains only letters, numbers, and hyphens.

Parent Category

None ⬍

Categories, unlike tags, can have a hierarchy. You might have a Jazz category, and under that have children categories for Bebop and Big Band. Totally optional.

Description

The description is not prominent by default; however, some themes may show it.

Add New Category

- The new "WordPress News" category should appear in the right hand side of the screen:

Categories

Add New Category

Name

The name is how it appears on your site.

Slug

The "slug" is the URL-friendly version of the name. It is usually all lowercase and contains only letters, numbers, and hyphens.

Parent Category

None

Categories, unlike tags, can have a hierarchy. You might have a Jazz category, and under that have children categories for Bebop and Big Band. Totally optional.

Description

Bulk Actions ⭥ Apply

☐ Name

☐ WordPress News

☐ Events

☐ — African Events

☐ — Asian Events

☐ — European Events

☐ — North American Events

- Go to "Add New Category".
- Name: **Plugin News**
- Parent Category: **WordPress News**
- Click "Add New Category".
- Repeat the process for categories called "Theme News" and "Official Releases".

☐ Name

☐ WordPress News

☐ — Official Releases

☐ — Theme News

☐ — Plugin News

Great! You now have ten different categories for your content. However, only categories that have posts will be visible on the site.

- Visit the front of your site and look on the right-hand side. Only categories that are being used are shown in the "Categories" widget:

CATEGORIES

European Events

Events

Wordville

You don't have to use categories, you can simply make one category for all your posts and then remove the "Categories" widget from the sidebar. Then categories simply become irrelevant on your site. However, once you have a large number of posts, categories are a good idea because they help people find related content.

CREATING TAGS

In this section, we are going to look at tags, which are another feature you can use to organize your content. It's easy to get confused about the difference between categories and tags, and honestly to a certain extent you can use them however you want. Let's look at how I recommend you use them.

- Go to edit the post, "WordCamp Europe in Belgrade".
- Under "Categories", the post is placed under "Events" and then "European Events", as shown in the next image.

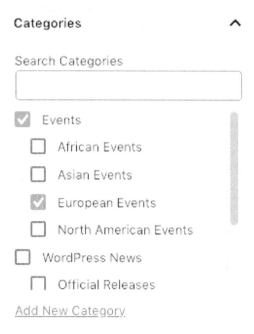

Below the "Categories" section, you see a "Tags" box. Tags are words associated with the post that you might want somebody to find when they are searching your site. However, tags are not common enough to be used as categories.

- Enter "WordCamp Europe" and click "Add".

- You'll see the tag added below the box. If you make a mistake, simply click on the cross next to the tag to delete it.

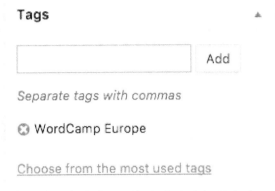

- Repeat the process with "Belgrade", "Serbia", "WordCamps", "Networking", and "Presentations".

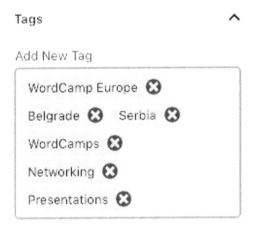

With tags, we're using a freeform textbox to add new tags. There is not a parent relationship as there is with categories. Tags cannot be organized into any logical hierarchy.

However, tags appear on your site in almost exactly the same way as categories.

- Save your post and visit the front of your site.
- Scroll down, and you'll see your new tags are presented next

to the categories. From here we could click on each individual tag, and it would show us all the different posts that are associated with that tag.

EUROPEAN EVENTS, EVENTS

\# BELGRADE, NETWORKING, PRESENTATIONS, SERBIA, WORDCAMP EUROPE, WORDCAMPS

At the moment, unlike categories, you can't see the tags in the sidebar of your site.

- On the front of your site, click "Customize" in the header menu.

- Click "Widgets" and then "Blog Sidebar".

- You'll see the widgets that are currently live on your site:

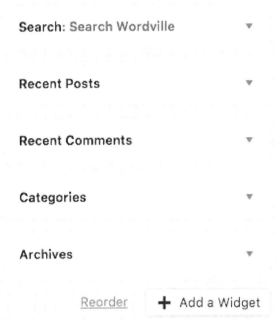

- Click the "Add a Widget" button.
- Click "Tag Cloud".

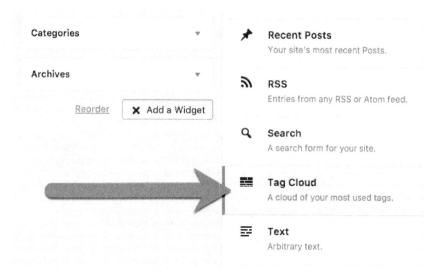

- You'll see that "Tag Cloud" has now been added to your sidebar:

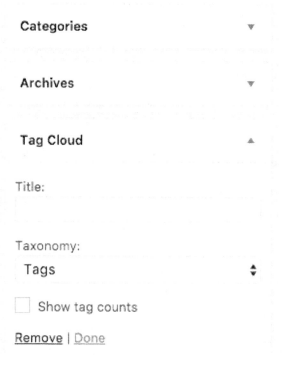

- Click "Publish".

- Click the "X" icon to leave this screen.

- Visit the front of your site, and you'll now see the Tag Cloud widget in your sidebar:

CATEGORIES

European Events

Events

Wordville

ARCHIVES

November 2017

TAGS

Belgrade   Networking   Presentations

Serbia   WordCamp Europe

WordCamps

MANAGING TAGS

Tags can be managed almost identically to categories.

- Click on the "Tags" link in the left menu, and you'll see an almost identical layout, with the exception of the missing "Parent" option when creating tags.

This works very much like the "Categories" page.

- There is a "Bulk Action" menu, but the only option it gives us is to delete. You can use this action to delete a number of tags all at once.

- Over on the right, there is a "Count" column that displays how many posts are in each tag. Click on the number to see posts only in that tag.

- You can also add new tags from this page very quickly, just as you can with the "Categories" page.

WHAT'S NEXT?

So far in this book, we've focused almost all our attention on posts.

However, we've seen that you can also create pages. Many WordPress sites don't require frequently updated content and rely heavily on pages.

In the next chapter, we'll take a close look at how you can use pages to build your WordPress site.

CHAPTER 6.

WORDPRESS PAGES EXPLAINED

In this chapter, we are going to take a look at pages in WordPress.

This is the point at which your WordPress site moves away from being a blog and starts to become a real website.

After reading this chapter, you will be able to:

- Choose a custom homepage and a news page.
- Create a menu, and add pages to the menu.
- Set up parent and child pages.
- Create a dropdown menu of pages.

CREATING PAGES

One of the first things that we are going to do is build a homepage. Then we'll move our Wordville news to a news page.

Let's take a look at how to do that. In the admin area on the left sidebar, there is a "Pages" section. You may already have two pages: "About Wordville" and "Sample Page".

We don't need a page on the site called "Sample Page", so let's rename and repurpose that page.

- Click "Edit" under "Sample Page".
- Change the title to "Wordville Location".

You can now clean up the text in this page:

- Delete all the existing blocks, except for the first Paragraph block. As a reminder, you can delete blocks by clicking the three-dot icon in the top-right corner and then clicking "Remove Block".

- Enter this new text: **Wordville is a place with a wonderful community. Come and move here. You'll agree that Wordville is a very enjoyable place to live.**

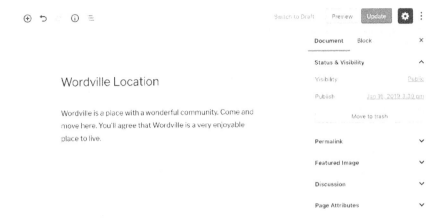

Take a step back now and look at the whole page. What's missing compared to the posts you created earlier?

What differences did you spot?

- There are no Categories.
- There are no Tags.
- Several boxes are missing from the right sidebar.

By design, the pages are much simpler than the posts you created earlier. In an earlier chapter, we mentioned that pages also don't have author names, publishing dates, or comments enabled by default.

My advice is to use pages for content that will not change very often.

SETTING YOUR HOMEPAGE AND NEWS PAGE

One good example of a page that may not change very often is your homepage. Some busy sites may update their homepage constantly, but many other websites go months without updating their homepage.

In this exercise, let's see how to use pages to create a new homepage.

- On the "All Pages" screen, click "Add New".
- Create and publish a page called "Homepage".
- Create and publish a page called "Wordville News".
- Your "All Pages" screen will now look like this:

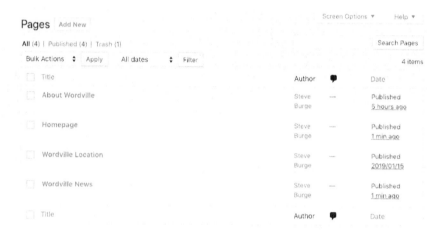

WordPress has a special way of deciding which page gets to be the homepage.

- Go into "Appearance", then "Customize".
- Click "Homepage Settings".

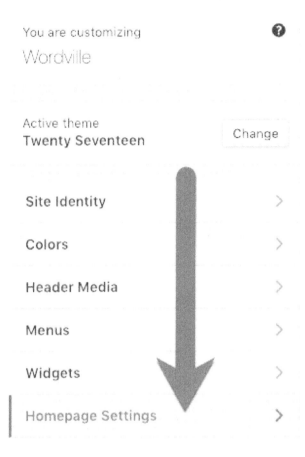

On this screen, you can choose the options for the homepage.

From the "Homepage" dropdown menu here, you can choose which page will be the front page of your website, as shown in the image below.

- Set the "Homepage" option to "Homepage".
- Set the "Posts page" option to "Wordville News".

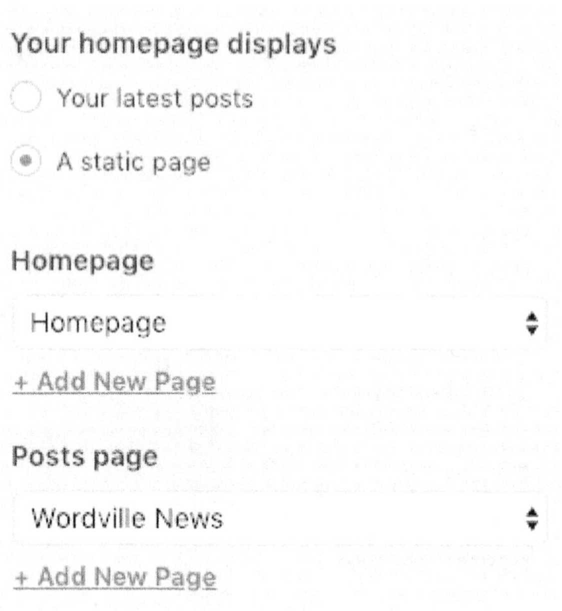

Your homepage displays

◯ Your latest posts

⊙ A static page

Homepage

| Homepage | ⬍ |

+ Add New Page

Posts page

| Wordville News | ⬍ |

+ Add New Page

- Click the blue "Publish" button.
- Go back to the "All Pages" screen, and you'll see that both pages are labelled with those new settings:

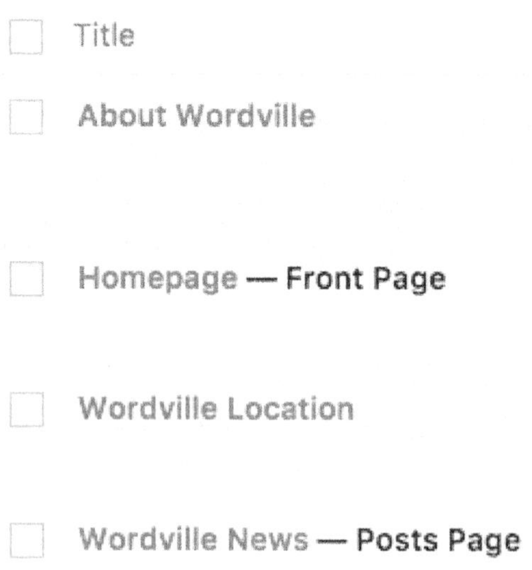

☐ Title

☐ About Wordville

☐ Homepage — **Front Page**

☐ Wordville Location

☐ Wordville News — **Posts Page**

- Click "View" for the "Wordville News" page, and you should see a list of all your posts.
- Click "View" for the "Homepage" page, and you should see a blank screen like the one below.

HOMEPAGE
Edit

Proudly powered by WordPress

ADDING PAGES TO MENUS

Using the steps above, we now have control over our homepage and our news page.

However, there's something missing – those pages aren't easily visible.

We need to make sure that our pages can be easily found.

- On the front of your site, click "Customize" in the admin toolbar.
- Click "Menus" in the left sidebar:

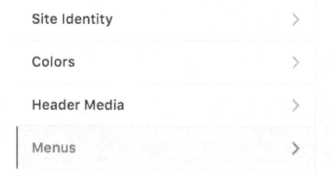

- WordPress will offer you the chance to create a menu for your links. Click "Create New Menu":

Menus

It doesn't look like your site has any menus yet. Want to build one? Click the button to start.

You'll create a menu, assign it a location, and add menu items like links to pages and categories. If your theme has multiple menu areas, you might need to create more than one.

Create New Menu

- Menu Name: **Main Menu**
- Menu Location: **Top Menu**
- Click "Next".

Menu Name

Main Menu

If your theme has multiple menus, giving them
clear names will help you manage them.

Menu Locations

Where do you want this menu to appear?
*(If you plan to use a menu widget, skip this
step.)*

☑ Top Menu

☐ Social Links Menu

Click "Next" to start adding links to your new
menu.

| Next |

Now you've successfully created a menu for your links. The next
step is to put the links into the menu.

- Click "Add Items".

Menu Name

Main Menu

Time to add some links! Click "Add menu
items" to start putting pages, categories, and
custom links in your menu. Add as many
things as you'd like.

+ Add Items

- Click the "+" icons next to "Homepage", "Wordville News", "About Wordville", and "Wordville Location".

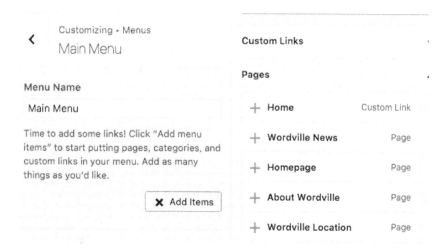

- As you add those menu links, you will start to see them appear on the left-hand side of the screen:

- Click "Publish" to save your changes. You now have a navigation menu that shows your pages so that visitors can find them easily.

PARENT AND CHILD PAGES

One of the key differences between posts and pages is the idea of parent and child pages.

This is signficantly different from the parent and child categories we used for posts. Here's a short explanation of the differences:

- A post can be assigned to multiple categories, including both a parent and a child category.

- A page can only be either a parent or a child page, and it can only be linked to one other page.

Let's see how the Parent / Child system works for pages.

In this exercise, we'll build an "Attractions" page that is linked to pages for the Wordville Aquarium, Zoo and Museum.

In the Resources folder that you downloaded, you'll find text for all these pages inside a file called attractions-text.txt.

- Go to the "All Pages" screen.

- Create and save a page called "Attractions".

- Create and save a page called "Aquarium".

- In the "Page Attributes" box of the "Aquarium" page, choose "Attractions" from the "Parent" dropdown:

- Create a page called "Museum" and choose "Attractions" as the "Parent".

- Create a page called "Zoo" and choose "Attractions" as the "Parent".

- Once you've saved your pages, visit the "All Pages" screen, and it should look like the image below. You can see that the child pages are indented:

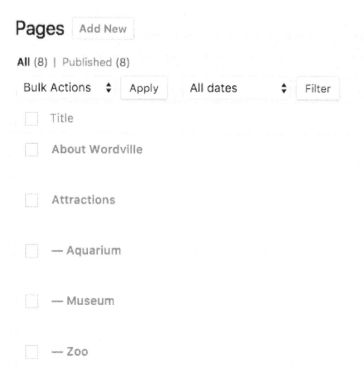

This is a noticeably less flexible system than the one we saw with categories. However, it's one of the best things we can do to organize pages.

In the chapter called "WordPress Plugins Explained", we'll show you how to add plugins. Some plugins offer the ability to show these child pages in useful ways on your site.

However, for now, let's use the following approach to show these child pages on your site.

- Click the "Customize" button in the admin menu, or go to "Appearance" and then "Customize".

- Click "Menus".

- Click "Main Menu".

- Click "Add Items".

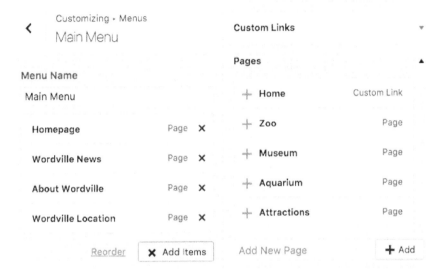

- Drag-and-drop the "Attractions", "Aquarium", "Museum", and "Zoo" pages from the right-hand column to go underneath the "Main Menu" links in the left-hand column.

- When you have added the pages to the left-hand column, you can drag-and-drop the links to reorder them. Rearrange the links so that the individual attractions are indented under the main "Attractions" page:

Menu Name

Main Menu

Homepage	Page	✕
Wordville News	Page	✕
About Wordville	Page	✕
Wordville Location	Page	✕
Attractions	Page	✕
Aquarium	Page	✕
Museum	Page	✕
Zoo	Page	✕

- Scroll over to the right side of the screen, and you should see that you now have a dropdown menu for your main "Attractions" page and child pages!

- Don't forget to hit "Publish" when you're finished.

Why did we cover menu links in this chapter called "WordPress Pages Explained"? We covered them here because it is difficult for people to see your pages unless you add them to a menu. It is the combination of pages and menus together that allows you to turn a basic WordPress blog into a real WordPress site.

WHAT'S NEXT?

At this point in the book, your Wordville site should look like the image below. Don't worry if your site doesn't match this exactly. If you understand the concepts we've covered so far, you're ready to move on.

At the moment, you have a lot of text and images. In the next chapter, you're going to discover how WordPress handles videos, audio, photo galleries and more dynamic content. Your site's content will be a lot more lively by the end of the next chapter!

Homepage   Wordville News   About Wordville   Wordville Location   Attractions ⌄   ↓

HOMEPAGE
Edit

Proudly powered by WordPress

CHAPTER 7.

WORDPRESS MEDIA AND GALLERIES EXPLAINED

In this chapter, we are going to talk about the Media Library that is built intoWordPress. The Media Library allows you to store images, music, and videos that you can use anywhere on your site.

After reading this chapter, you will be able to:

- Edit images.
- Create photo galleries.
- Upload your own video and audio files.
- Understand more about media embeds in WordPress.

EDITING IMAGES

In the left sidebar, click "Media" and you will be taken to your Media Library. This is where all the images, videos, audio files, and other media is stored for your site.

Currently, you have several images in the Media Library, including images used in your posts and in customizing the look of your site.

In the Media Library, you can search for items, filter them by type or date, and you can rearrange how they are displayed.

However, you can also upload and edit media from this page too. WordPress really does have some powerful options for working with images, so let's see them in action.

- Click "Add New" and then "Select Files".

- Upload the wapuu.png file from the "Resources" folder you downloaded. Wapuu is the WordPress mascot. You can find many different kinds of Wapuu at https://wapu.us/wapuus/.

- Click on the image after it has uploaded:

- You can now see the file name, the file type, when it was uploaded, the file size and the image's dimensions. You can also see the URL of the image, and you have the ability to set a Title, Caption, Alt Text and Description. I recommend always putting in at least the Alt text. This makes it easier for people with screen readers to know what's going on in your images.

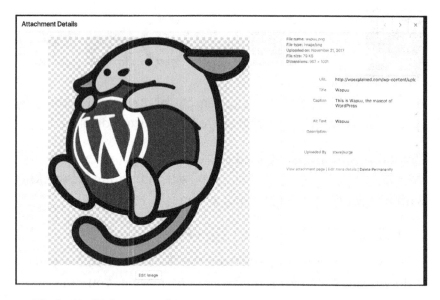

- Click the "Edit Image" link underneath the image:

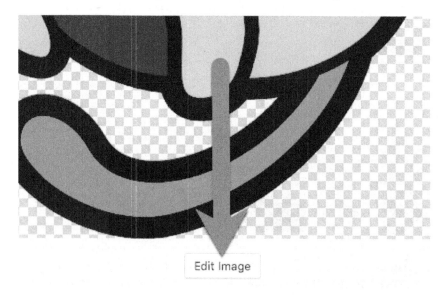

- On this next screen, look at the tools over your image. Using these buttons, you can crop, rotate, and flip your image.

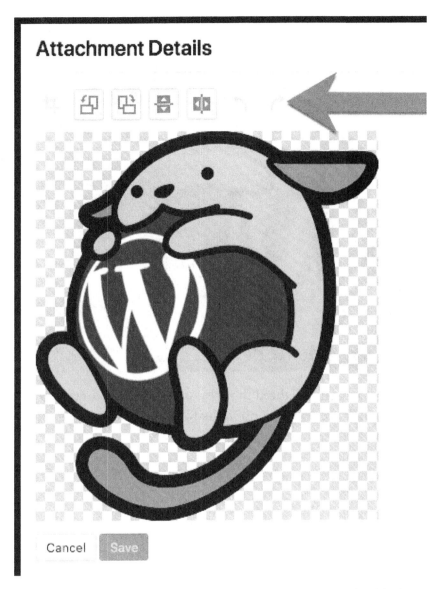

- If you want to crop your image, use your cursor to highlight an area of the image. You can do this by clicking your mouse over your image and then dragging the cursor to create a box, as in the screenshot below:

- Once you've highlighted the area of the image you want to keep, click the "Crop" icon in the top-left corner, as shown below.

- You can rotate and flip your image using the other buttons. For example, click the "Rotate Left" button twice to turn your Wapuu upside down:

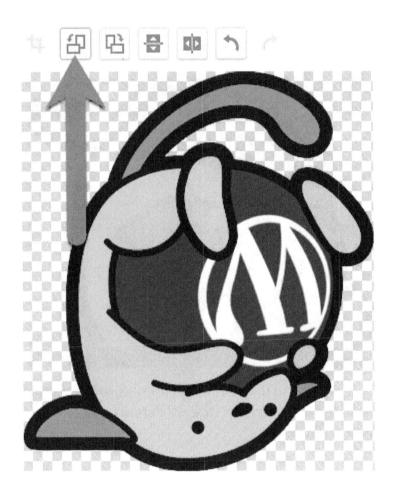

- Over on the right side, you can change the size of the image, using the "Scale Image" and "Image Crop" options:

SCALE IMAGE ❷

Original dimensions 907 × 1001

New dimensions:

907 × 1001 **Scale**

IMAGE CROP ❷

Aspect ratio:

:

Selection:

×

THUMBNAIL SETTINGS ❷

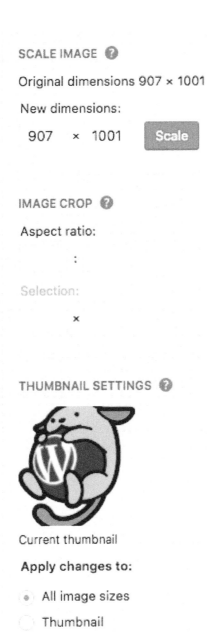

Current thumbnail

Apply changes to:

◉ All image sizes

◯ Thumbnail

◯ All sizes except thumbnail

- Notice at the bottom that WordPress allows you to "Apply changes to" different image sizes.

When you upload an image, WordPress actually makes multiple

sizes of it. By default, WordPress makes a "Thumbnail", "Medium", and "Large" size. These sizes are defined under "Settings" and "Media".

Media Settings

Image sizes

The sizes listed below determine the maximum dimensions in pixels to use when adding an image to the Media Library.

Thumbnail size	Width 150	Height 150
	☑ Crop thumbnail to exact dimensions (normally thumbnails are proportional)	
Medium size	Max Width 300	Max Height 300
Large size	Max Width 1024	Max Height 1024

Every time you upload an image, it creates a thumbnail, medium, and large size. These are maximum heights, so if you have an image that is wider than it is tall, it will keep the aspect ratio and won't always give you square images. It also maintains the original size, so you can work with it later if you need to.

You can choose between the different image sizes when you place images into content. Let's see how that works:

- Go to "Pages" and then "Zoo".
- Click the + icon and add a new Image block.
- Click the "Media Library" button.

The zoo also has exotic animals such as a wapuu. A wapuu is a cuddly yellow that looks

Image

Drag an image, upload a new one or select a file from your library.

Upload   Media Library

Insert from URL

- Choose the Wapuu image.
- Click "Select" and you can see your image added to your content:

Zoo

Wordville Zoo is a wonderful place for families to visit.

There is an aviary for birds and a farm for animals like cows, pigs and geese.

The zoo also has exotic animals such as a wapuu. A wapuu is a cuddly yellow that looks like a bear.

- You'll notice that the image is really large. You can change the size of the image using the settings in the right sidebar. In this example below, I've chosen "Medium " for the "Image Size".

- I've also added "Alt Text" which is recommended for search engines. It's also helpful for peope with less than perfect eyesight who may have a device that reads webpages for them.

- It is also possible to grab the corners of the image and drag it to stretch the image larger:

Write caption...

CREATING PHOTO GALLERIES

WordPress allows you to upload, manage and display single images. You can also do the same for multiple images at the same time.

Earlier we built a page for the Aquarium, but we didn't put anything on it, except for text. In this exercise, we are going to create a really cool photo gallery for our Aquarium page.

- Go to "Pages" and edit the "Aquarium" page.
- Click the + icon and add a "Gallery" block.
- Click the "Upload" button in the new block.

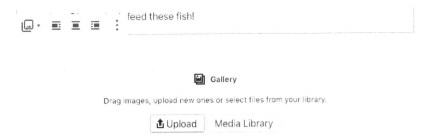

- Upload all six images from the /aquarium-gallery/ folder in the Resources folder you downloaded.

- WordPress will automatically turn those images into a gallery. WordPress is smart enough to try and use data in the images to create a caption. In this example, that has worked for 4 of the 6 images:

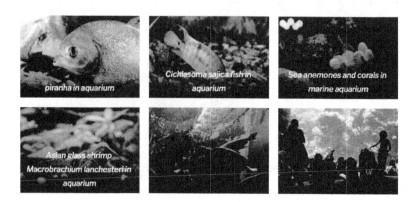

- In the right sidebar, you can tweak options for the gallery. For example, you can change how many columns are shown in the gallery.

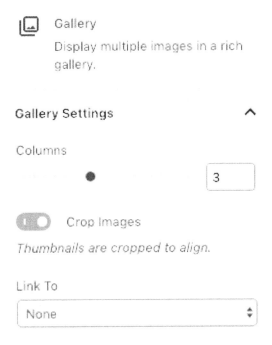

- Save the page, visit the front of your site, and you can see your new photo gallery in action!

One of the great things aboutWordPress photo galleries is that while they are very simple, they are extremely extendable. There are dozens of plugins that can do wonderful things with this gallery. You can make slideshows, zoom effects, and all sorts of other cool things.

UPLOADING YOUR OWN VIDEO AND AUDIO FILES

In the next part of this chapter, we're going to upload your own multimedia files. Earlier in the book, we used videos from YouTube. This time we're going to use our own files.

- Go to "Posts" and click "Add New".
- Title: **Wordville Concert in the Park**
- Paragraph block: **Wordville is holding an event for local families. Join us for movies and music.**
- Categories: **Wordville**
- Featured Image: Use the concert-featured-image.jpg file from the /concert-multimedia/ file in the Resources folder.

Now we're going to upload a video file:

- Add a "Video" block.
- Click the "Upload" button.
- Upload the file called movie.mp4 from the /concert-multimedia/ file in the Resources folder.
- You'll now see the video directly inside your post:

Wordville Concert in the Park

for local families. Join us for movies and music.

Write caption...

The video will not play in your admin area, but it will work on the front of your site.

- Publish this post and have a look at the front-end of your site. You will have a working movie:

Wordville Concert in the Park

Wordville is holding an event for local families. Join us for movies and music.

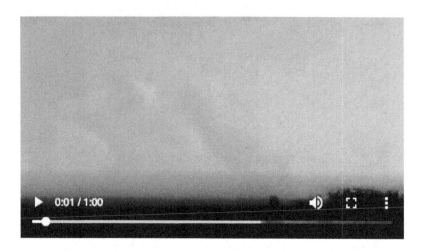

🔖 **WORDVILLE**

Edit

Let's go back to edit the post and see how WordPress handles audio.

- Go back to editing the "Wordville Concert in the Park" post.

- Add an "Audio" block.

- Click on the "Upload" button.

- Upload the audio file from the /concert-multimedia/ folder in the Resources folder.

- You'll now see that WordPress is ready to play that audio file:

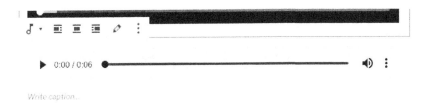

As with the video, this audio file won't play in your admin area. Click "Update" and then "View Post" to listen to this music.

MORE ADVANCED EMBEDS

Earlier in the book, you took YouTube URLs and used those embed videos in your site. WordPress supports a wide range of sites beyond just YouTube, and you can use this feature to share all sorts of media on your site.

When you add a new block, look for the "Embeds" section. WordPress supports Twitter, Facebook, Instagram, SoundCloud, Spotify, Flickr and many other sites.

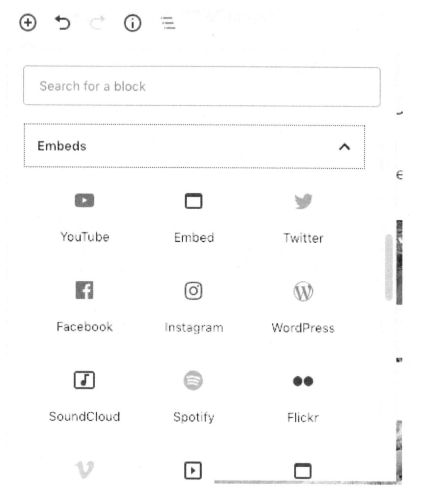

Let's use Twitter as an example of how these embeds work:

- Go to http://twitter.com/wordpress.
- Click the date of the lastest post from the WordPress team:

WordPress ✔ @WordPress · 6 Dec, 2018
WordPress 5.0 "Bebo" wordpress. /news/2018/12/b...

Welcome to WordPress)

Of Mountains
& Printing Presses

○ 171 ⟳ 631 ♡ 752 ✉

- Copy the URL of this tweet. In this example, the URL is https://twitter.com/WordPress/status/930967986038591489.

- Go to "Posts" and then "Add New".

- Title: **WordPress 5.0 is Here!**

- Paragraph text: **The WordPress team have just released the latest WordPress update.**

- Featured Image: Use the file wordpress-release-featured-image.jpg from the Resources folder.

- Paste the URL for the tweet into the body, and you'll see the complete tweet.

WordPress 5.0 is Here!

The WordPress team have just released the latest WordPress update.

WordPress 5.0 "Bebo" https://t.co/hW9nfThfiB pic.twitter.com/KJP5v3YBnv

— WordPress (@WordPress) December 6, 2018

- Publish your post and visit the front of your site. The tweet should be embedded into your content and look beautiful!

FEBRUARY 3, 2019 BY STEVE BURGE

WordPress 5.0 is Here!

The WordPress team have just released the latest WordPress update.

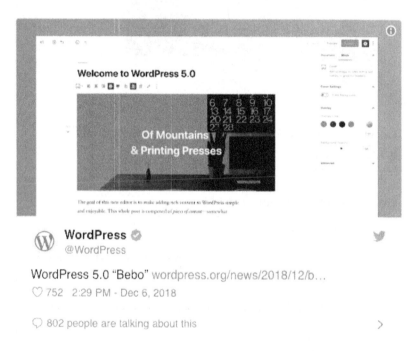

This embed feature can be a wonderful way to include content from around the internet on your site. Being able to embed video, social media posts, and photos from over 30 popular websites can really enhance your site.

WHAT'S NEXT?

During the first few chapters of this book, you've seen many of the important features that are included with WordPress. All those chapters have been part of Step 2 in our WordPress workflow: content.

In the next chapter, we're going to move on to Step 3: Plugins. We're going to explore adding new features to your site. Turn the page, and let's investigate the world of plugins.

1. Planning

2. Content

3. Plugins

4. Design

5. Users

6. Launch

7. Maintenance

CHAPTER 8.

WORDPRESS PLUGINS EXPLAINED

In this chapter, we are going to take a look at WordPress plugins. Plugins are extra code that you can add to your site to add extra features. Fortunately plugins are packaged very nicely, so it makes it super easy to add and remove plugins.

After reading this chapter, you will be able to:

- Find plugins.
- Install and use plugins.
- Analyze plugins.
- Disable and delete plugins.

FINDING PLUGINS

First, let's go to WordPress.org and see what kind of plugins are available. The image below shows http://wordpress.org/plugins. When I took this screenshot, there were over 53,000 plugins available!

In the "Featured Plugins" area, the first plugin we see is Akismet, which is already installed on our site. Akismet can protect your site from spam. Next to Akismet is a plugin called Jetpack, which provides 101 different features, from statistics and SEO to improved photo and video galleries. WP Super Cache makes your site run more quickly. bbPress adds a discussion forum to your site.

Featured Plugins

See all

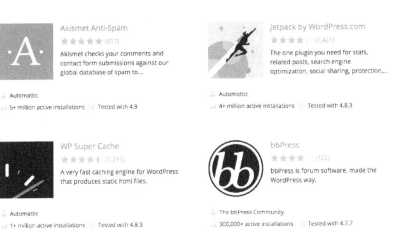

The easiest way to start exploring the plugin directory is with the search box.

- Type in keywords that describe the kind of plugin you're

looking for. For example, type in "business directory" if you want to add details of businesses based in Wordville:

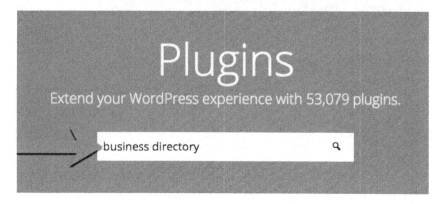

- This next image shows the result of that search. Many of these plugins have over 10,000 users and have very high ratings. There are a lot of good choices here, and in this situation you might test several of them to find the right choice for your site.

Showing results for: **business directory**

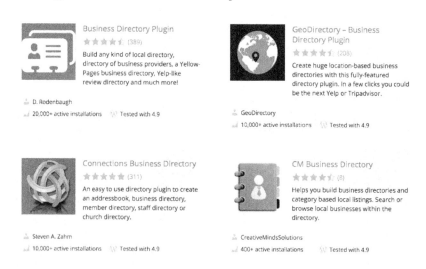

- Click on one plugin's title, and you'll find a page with complete details on that plugin:

Business Directory Plugin
By D. Rodenbaugh

Download

Details   Reviews   Installation   Support   Development

Description

Main Site | Support | Docs | Showcase | Premium Modules

Business Directory Plugin is the most popular, versatile, widely-installed, easiest to use, and best-supported WordPress Business Directory plugin available. Increase interaction on your website, improve customer retention and a add revenue-generating section to your site with Business Directory Plugin!

Version:	5.1.2
Last updated:	10 hours ago
Active installations:	20,000+
Requires WordPress Version:	4.3
Tested up to:	4.9
Requires PHP Version:	5.6

So there are over 53,000 plugins, and there's a large directory which allows you to search through them all.

Did you know that all this information is available without leaving your site?

- Go to "Plugins" and then "Add New".

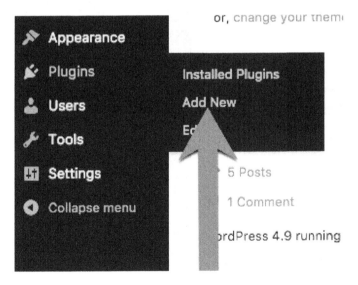

- You will find all the same plugins that you saw on WordPress.org. On the first screen, you'll see the same four "Featured" plugins in exactly the same order:

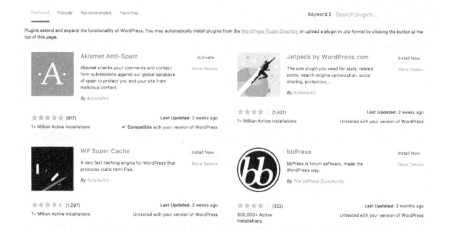

INSTALLING PLUGINS

To install a plugin, all you have to do is click the "Install Now" button for a plugin. Look at the image above, and you can see the "Install Now" buttons are displayed throughout the plugin directory.

Let's take you through the process of installing and using a plugin. This exercise will allow us to add a calendar showing the content we've published.

- Search for "PublishPress".
- Click the "Install Now" button.

- Click the "Activate" button.

PublishPress – Professional publishing
tools for WordPress

Activate

More Details

PublishPress is the plugin for professional publishers. Get
an editorial calendar, flexible permissions and
notifications.

PublishPress

By PublishPress

★ ★ ★ ★ ★ (50)

1,000+ Active Installations

Last Updated: 4 days ago

✓ Compatible with your version of WordPress

- And now your plugin is active. If you click the "Plugins" link, you'll see your new plugin sitting next to Akismet and Hello Dolly. On this screen you can quickly spot which plugins are active and which are not. Activated plugins are a light blue color, and have a solid blue vertical line on the left.

Now let's use our new plugin:

- Go to "PublishPress", then "Calendar".

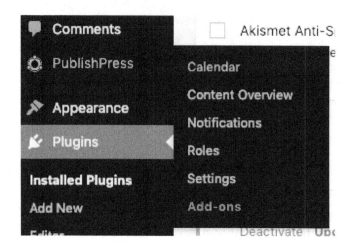

- You'll see a Calendar showing the recently published content on your site.

- If you want to publish this content on a different date, you can do that by dragging-and-dropping it to a new location in the calendar:

| All statuses ⇕ | All categories ⇕ | All tags ⇕ | All users ⇕ | All types ⇕ | 5 weeks ⇕ | Reset | | « ‹ Today › » |

Monday	Tuesday	Wednesday	Thursday	Friday	Saturday	Sunday
				January February		
28	29	30	31	1	2	3 ✓ WordPress 5.0 is He... ✓ Wordville Concert in... ✓ Museum
4	5	6 ✓ Zoo	7	8	9	10
11	12	13	14	15	16	17

ANALYZING PLUGINS

Something important to remember is that not all plugins are created equal in terms of quality.

Some plugins are excellent software with high-quality code and have an excellent user interface. Other plugins are written poorly and can be difficult to use. The WordPress team can't perform detailed checks on over 53,000 plugins, so you'll need to take some time to analyze plugins before and after installing them.

Let's take a look at a plugin called Ninja Forms that we'll use in the next chapter.

• Go to "Plugins" and then "Add New".

• Search for "Ninja Forms".

Ninja Forms – The Easy and Powerful Forms Builder

Install Now

More Details

Drag and drop fields in an intuitive UI to create contact forms, email subscription forms, order forms, payment forms, send emails and more!

By The WP Ninjas

 (842)

Last Updated: 2 weeks ago

1+ Million Active Installations   Untested with your version of WordPress

- Click the "More Details" link in the top-right corner.
- You will be taken to a new window that looks like the image below.

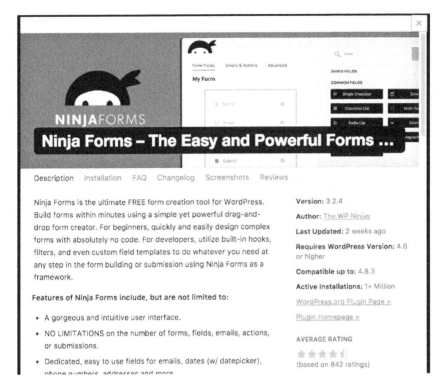

Take a look at some of the key information about Ninja Forms:

- Last Updated: 2 weeks ago
- Active Installations: 1+ Million
- Average Rating: 4.5

All of these details lead us to think that this is a popular plugin that is well supported and people enjoy using.

In contrast to Ninja Forms, some plugins aren't supported and haven't been updated in quite a while. Let's take a look at how we can tell some of those things.

- Go to "Plugins" and then "Add New".
- Search for "Linkmarklet".
- Click the "More Details" link.

Linkmarklet

[ADOPT ME!] Linkmarklet
is an alternative to the
Press This! bookmarklet
aimed at rapid
linkblogging. Quickly post
while saving a link to a
Custom Fie ...

By Jonathan Christopher

Install Now

More Details

★ ★ ★ ★ ★ (3)

60+ Active Installs

Last Updated: 3 years ago

Untested with your version of WordPress

- You will be taken to a pop-up window that looks like the next image.

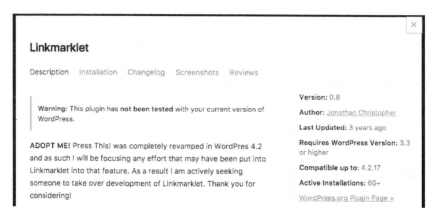

Notice the warning in the yellow area. It says:

Warning: This plugin has **not been tested** with your current version of WordPress.

The right sidebar shows us some useful information:

- The plugin was last updated 3 years ago.

- The plugin has only 60 active installs.

Before installing a plugin, make sure you read these details. They can help you decide whether a plugin is regularly updated and has been tested on your version of WordPress.

DEACTIVATING AND DELETING PLUGINS

If you find that you don't want a plugin, you can simply deactivate it and then delete it.

I do recommend that you delete any plugins that you decide not to use.

WordPress plugins that are not active can still be accessed from the web. This means that if the plugin has a security hole, then it can still be abused. It's common for people to deactivate a plugin but not delete it. I would recommend keeping things simple and removing any plugin that you don't need.

- To remove a plugin, click "Deactivate" on the "Plugins" screen:

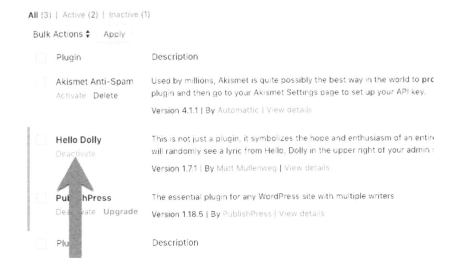

WHAT'S NEXT?

In the next chapter, we're going to explore plugins in more depth.

We're going to use the Ninja Forms plugin to create a contact form for your site.

People will be able to come to your site and send you messages. Ninja Forms will store that message, and they will also email a copy to you.

CHAPTER 9.

WORDPRESS CONTACT FORMS EXPLAINED

We are building this site for the city Wordville, and as a friendly community, it's great to get feedback from the people who live here.

In this chapter, we are going to set up a contact form. This will provide a way for the citizens of Wordville to get in contact with their local government.

After this chapter, you will be able to:

- Install a contact form plugin.
- Create a custom contact form.
- Publish and use a contact form.

INSTALLING A CONTACT FORM PLUGIN

For the contact form, we're going to use a plugin called Ninja Forms. In the last chapter, we saw that Ninja Forms has very positive reviews, over 1 million users, and is frequently updated.

- Go to "Plugins" and then "Add New".
- Search for "Ninja Forms".

Ninja Forms – The Easy and Powerful Forms Builder

Install Now

More Details

Drag and drop fields in an intuitive UI to create contact forms, email subscription forms, order forms, payment forms, send emails and more!

By *The WP Ninjas*

★★★★☆ (949)

1+ Million Active Installations

Last Updated: 2 weeks ago

✓ **Compatible** with your version of WordPress

- Click "Install Now" and then "Activate".
- Click "Ninja Forms" in the admin menu:

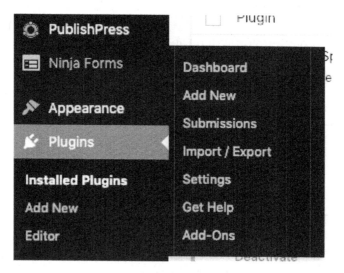

- You see a "Contact Me" form that has already been created.

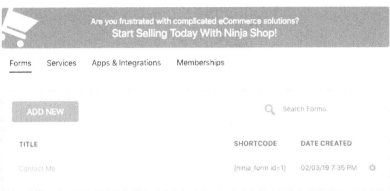

- Click the Title, which in this case is "Contact Me".
- You see that our form will have a place for people to leave their name, email and message before submitting.

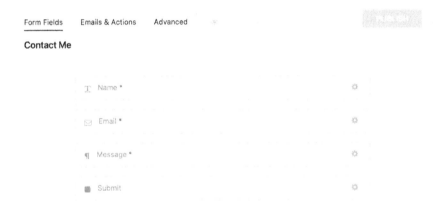

However, let's add another field so we can collect more details from people who contact us.

- Click the big, blue "+" button in the bottom right corner.

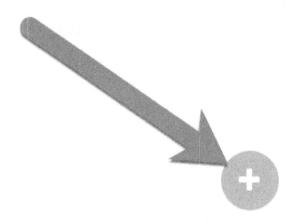

- You will now see a range of different fields, including "Single Checkbox", "Date", "Address", "City", "Email", "First Name", and more.

SAVED FIELDS

COMMON FIELDS

☑ Single Checkbox	📅 Date
☰ Checkbox List	☐ Multi-Select
⊙ Radio List	⌄ Select
▪ Submit	¶ Paragraph Text
T Single Line Text	

USER INFORMATION FIELDS

📍 Address	📍 City
✉ Email	👤 First Name
👤 Last Name	☐ Country
📍 US States	📞 Phone
📍 Zip	

- Drag the "Phone" field from the right column and move it into the left column. Make sure to drag it inside the blue-outlined box.

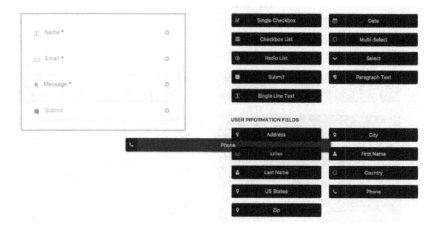

- You can place this new "Phone" field into the middle of the form:

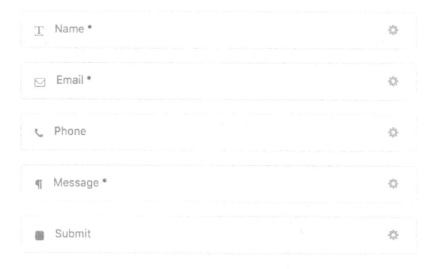

- If you click on the cog icon on the right of each field, it will open up a settings box for that specific field, as shown in the image below. Here you can control several key elements about this field, including the label that visitors will see and whether the field is required.

- Now that we have added a phone field, navigate to the "Emails & Actions" tab.

- Each of these rows is an action that takes place when the form is submitted. The first thing that it does is save the form submissions to the database.

- Click the cog next to "Email Confirmation". Here you can control the "Thank You" email that is sent to the user after they contact you.

- "Submission Confirmation" is a pretty bland subject line so, change it to say "Wordville Contact Confirmation".

- In the body area, write "Thank you for getting in touch with Wordville."

- The third option, "Email Notification", controls the email that is sent to you after the user sends a message.

- The final option, "Sucess Message", is the text users will see on the screen after contacting you. Let's personalize this text also to make it more friendly. If you want to include details from the form submission, click the "Table" icon shown below:

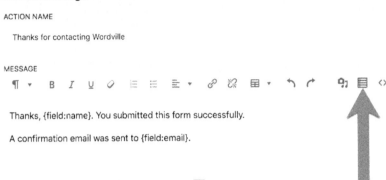

- The pop-up window will give you all the details you can use inside the form message. For example, to use the visitor's name in a message, you can use {field:name}.

- Here's an example of how to use that personalization, by placing {field:name} into the body:

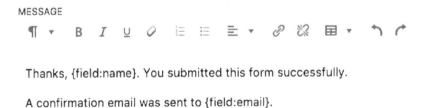

- Now let's go across to "Advanced" and then click on "Display Settings".
- Here you change the name of the form to "Contact Wordville".
- Click the "Done" button to save the new title.
- Click the "Publish" button to complete your changes to the form.

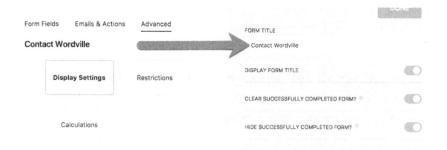

PUBLISHING AND USING THE CONTACT FORM

You now have a contact form, but it isn't available to your visitors yet.

Remember back to the chapter on photo galleries when we briefly showed you the shortcode that was used to create the galleries.

Ninja Forms has shortcodes too, and those can be used to place forms on our site. Copy-and-paste the shortcode for this form.

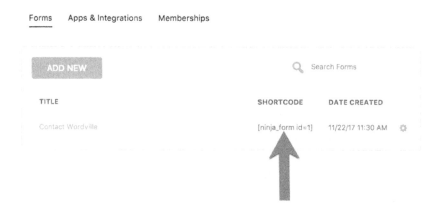

- Go to "Pages" and then "Add New".
- Place the shortcode into the page, as in the screen below.
- Click "Publish" twice.

Next, let's make it possible for people to access this new form:

- Go to "Customize", then "Menus", and then "Main Menu".
- Click "Add Items".
- Add "Contact Us" to your menu links.
- Click "Publish" to save the changes.

Menu Name		
Main Menu		
Homepage	Page	✕
Wordville News	Page	✕
About Wordville	Page	✕
Wordville Location	Page	✕
Attractions	Page	✕
Aquarium	Page	✕
Museum	Page	✕
Zoo	Page	✕
Contact Us	Page	✕

- Visit the front of your site, and you'll see your form in action.
- Try using the form. You have required fields, so if you try to submit empty fields, those required fields will turn red. So at a minimum you must put in your name, email, and our message.
- Fill out those fields and click "Submit".

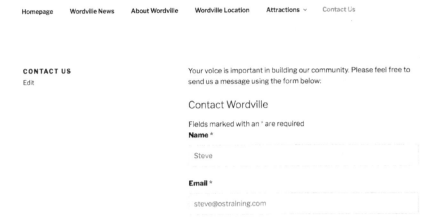

- Once you click "Submit", the form disappears and you see this success message:

  Thanks, Steve. You submitted this form successfully.

  A confirmation email was sent to steve@ostraining.com.

- To see the messages sent via your form, go to "Ninja Forms", then "Submissions" and select your form.

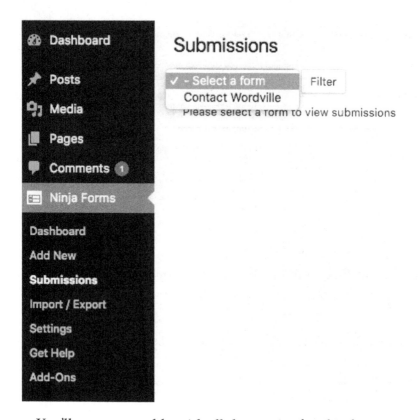

- You'll now see a table with all the entries for this form:

MAKING MONEY FROM PLUGINS

After seeing this free plugin, you might be asking yourself:

How is it possible that so many good plugins are available for free?

There are a variety of answers to this question. One alternative to Ninja Forms is called Contact Form 7. This hugely popular plugin is developed for free by Takayuki Miyoshi. He doesn't have a business model for the plugin. He simply loves to create good software and provide useful tools for people like you.

Contact Form 7

Install Now

Just another contact form plugin. Simple but flexible.

More Details

By Takayuki Miyoshi

★★★★☆ (1,422)

1+ Million Active Installations

Last Updated: 3 weeks ago

✔ **Compatible** with your version of WordPress

Other plugin developers also want to create good software and help people, but they don't have the luxury of working for free.

Plugins such as Ninja Forms are called "freemium". This means the main plugin is free, but you can purchase add-ons to do special custom things. If you visit https://ninjaforms.com/extensions/, you'll find a wide range of extra features that you can purchase. The sale of these add-ons allows the developer to pay for the costs involved in developing a plugin, and it also allows them to pay themselves a salary.

WHAT'S NEXT?

We've now finished Step 3 in our site-building process: Plugins.

In the next chapter, we're going to turn our attention to Step 4: Design.

Plugins add features to your site. Themes control the design, layout and style of your site.

1. **Planning**

2. **Content**

3. **Plugins**

4. **Design**

5. **Users**

6. **Launch**

7. **Maintenance**

CHAPTER 10.

WORDPRESS THEMES EXPLAINED

In this chapter, we're going to talk about themes for WordPress.

Themes are the most important factor in controlling how your site looks. Themes are installed in the same way as plugins, but there are some major differences. For example, many plugins can be installed and activated at the same time. Only a single theme can be active at one time.

After this chapter, you will be able to:

- Find themes.
- Install and use themes.
- Analyze themes.
- Disable and delete themes.

FINDING THEMES

So far in this book, we've been using a single theme. Let's see where that theme is located in our site:

- Go to "Appearance" and then "Themes".
- You'll see at least three themes (some hosting companies may add more themes).

These themes are released almost every year. We're using "Twenty Seventeen", for the simple reason that I prefer it and think it's more useful for beginners. The "Twenty Nineteen" theme is a little too plain and boring, in my humble opinion. Oh, and for the first time in many years, the WordPress team didn't release a theme in 2018 so there is no "Twenty Eighteen".

These themes are not really intended for professionally designed sites but are for demonstration purposes. They showcase many of the default features in WordPress and make a good starting point for beginners.

If you want to change the design of your site, the place to go is https://wordpress.org/themes/. This operates in a very similar way to the Plugin Directory we saw earlier in the book. There are 1,000's of themes to choose from, and all of them are free.

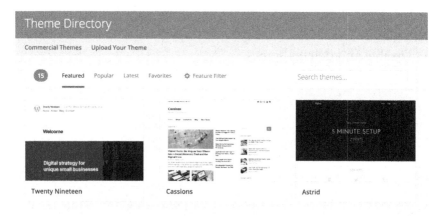

If you click on one of the themes, you get a better picture, as well as a description of the theme. The layout of these screens is slightly different from the plugins, but you'll see lots of the same details, including "Last updated", "Active Installs", and "Ratings".

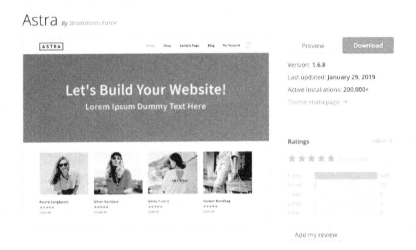

If you're looking for a particular kind of design, the "Feature Filter" will be very useful. For example, this allows you to select whether a theme has one, two, three, or four columns. You can also select what kind of style you want: blog, e-commerce, news, portfolio, or something different.

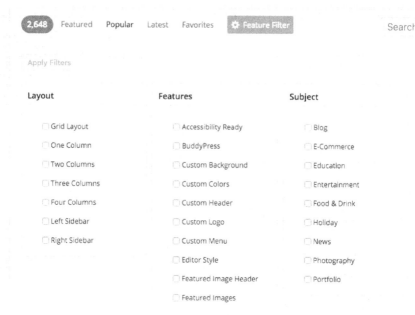

Layout	Features	Subject
☐ Grid Layout	☐ Accessibility Ready	☐ Blog
☐ One Column	☐ BuddyPress	☐ E-Commerce
☐ Two Columns	☐ Custom Background	☐ Education
☐ Three Columns	☐ Custom Colors	☐ Entertainment
☐ Four Columns	☐ Custom Header	☐ Food & Drink
☐ Left Sidebar	☐ Custom Logo	☐ Holiday
☐ Right Sidebar	☐ Custom Menu	☐ News
	☐ Editor Style	☐ Photography
	☐ Featured Image Header	☐ Portfolio
	☐ Featured Images	

In addition to all the free themes, there are also commercial themes: https://wordpress.org/themes/commercial/. These are themes that you pay for. They cannot be downloaded from WordPress.org or from within your WordPress site.

Commercially Supported GPL Themes

While our directory is full of fantastic themes, sometimes people want to use something that they know has support behind it, and don't mind paying for that. The GPL doesn't say that everything must be zero-cost, just that when you receive the software it must not restrict your freedoms in how you use it.

With that in mind, here are a collection of folks who provide GPL themes with extra paid services available around them. Some of them you may pay to access, some of them are membership sites, some may give you the theme for zero-cost and just charge for support. What they all have in common is people behind them who support open source, WordPress, and its GPL license.

Axle Themes   ThemeZee   Themes Harbor

Notice the detailed description on top of this page? "GPL" is the license used for WordPress code. It says that it's fine to charge people for your code, but you can't restrict what they do with that code. In many cases, what you actually pay for from these commercial theme providers is support. They can help you to get the theme configured properly and whenever you get stuck.

What's different about commercial themes is that usually you buy them and then download a compressed file. To install commercial themes, you go to the "Themes" page, click "Add New" and use the "Upload Theme" button.

INSTALLING THEMES

Let's go through the process of installing a free theme. This process is very similar to installing plugins.

- Go to "Appearance" and then "Themes".

- Click "Add New".

- As you are searching for a theme, you can see what they may look like on your site. Click the "Preview" button:

- For our Wordville site, we're going to use a theme called Astra. Search for "Astra".

- Click "Install" and then "Activate":

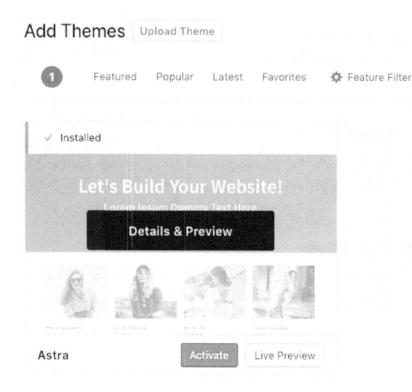

- Click the "Customize" button for Astra:

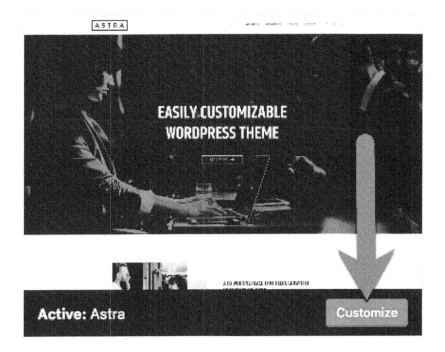

- You will now see Astra inside the Customizer area:

The options contained within the Customizer do vary from theme to theme. Some themes have dozens of options here, and some themes have just a few.

The next step in our site-building process will be to use the Customizer to design the Astra theme. Let's walk through the steps one-by-one until we get a great-looking site.

None of these changes go live until you click "Publish". The Customizer allows you to make changes and view them in your own site with your own content before committing those changes.

- Click "Layout", then "Header", then "Site Identity".
- For the logo, upload the wordville-logo.png file from /astra-redesign in the Resources folder. Don't crop the logo when you upload it.
- Uncheck the box "Display Site Title".
- Modify the "Logo Width" option until the logo fits nicely on your site:

- For the Site Icon option, you can use the same image we chose earlier in the book for the Twenty Seventeen theme. That file was called wordville-logo.png. You might have noticed that we now have two images called wordville-logo.png. WordPress does not have a problem with that and you can safely upload multiple files with the same name.

Next, let's update the color scheme to match our site's logo:

- Click the back arrow next to "Site Identity".
- Click the back arrow next to "Header".
- Click the "Colors & Background" link.
- Click "Base Colors"
- Change "Theme Color" to a new color: #d54f22. This is the same orange color used in the logo:

Base Colors

Theme Color

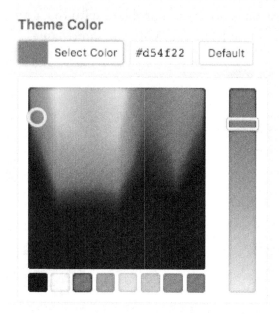

- Change the "Link Color" to #d54f22 also.

Base Colors

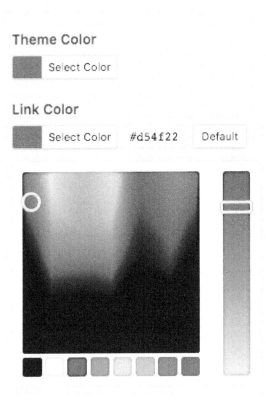

Theme Color

Select Color

Link Color

Select Color   #d54f22   Default

One thing you may notice is that there's less room for the menu in this theme, compared to the previous theme. If you narrow your browser window, you'll see that your menu will break onto a new row when the width is too narrow:

We can fix this problem by tweaking the text in the menu links to make them shorter.

- Click "Menus" and then "Main Menu".

- Inside each menu link, shorten the title. For example, "Homepage" can be reduced to "Home".

- After updating each menu link, click the up arrow in the top-right corner of the box to minimize the settings for that link.

- Keep doing this until all your menu links use just a single word:

What else can we do to use the Astra theme as well as possible? We can certainly improve the footer area.

- Click the back arrow next to "Menus" so you go up to the top level of the settings.

- Click "Layout", then "Footer", then "Footer Widgets".

- Choose the four column layout for the footer:

- Click the back arrow so you go up to the top level of the settings.
- Click "Widgets".
- You'll now see four footer areas:

- Open each of the four widget areas and add a widget. I have some suggestions for you in the screenshot below, but at this point you should be feeling more confident in your own judgement about WordPress. Use this opportunity to experiment with different widgets:

Finally, you might want to improve the footer which contains the copyright information at the very bottom of the page.

- Click the pencil icon shown below:

You can use this opportunity to remove the "Powered by Astra" text if you don't find that useful:

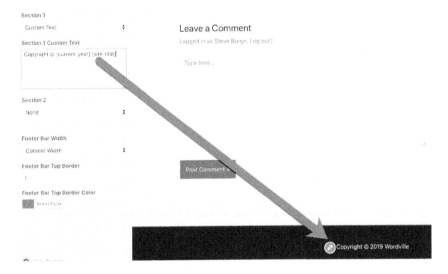

Section 1
  Custom Text   Leave a Comment
Section 1 Custom Text   Logged in as Steve Burge. Log out?
  Copyright @ [current year] [site_title]
                                              Type here..
Section 2
  None

Footer Bar Width
  Content Width

Footer Bar Top Border
  1   Post Comment
Footer Bar Top Border Color
    Select Color
                                                            Copyright © 2019 Wordville

As with the widgets, feel free to play around with Astra's settings. Do some experimentation and see which features you like.

- Remember that none of your changes will be saved until you click "Publish".

HOW TO CHOOSE GOOD THEMES

Themes are what make your site look the way it does. So, for many WordPress users, the theme is the most important aspect of their site, and it's important to choose carefully.

There are many free themes at WordPress.org, and there are some excellent commercial options that are linked to from WordPress.org.

It is also possible to create a custom theme. If you're a coder, you can learn to build your own themes. If you're not interested in development, you can hire someone to build a theme that is exactly customized for your site's needs.

I would recommend reading more about this topic to see all the features that determine the quality of a theme. You can find

links and reading suggestions at: https://ostraining.com/books/
wordpress/themes/.

WHAT'S NEXT?

You may have noticed that our site looks good, but our homepage
does not. In fact, our homepage is completely blank!

In the next chapter, we're going to show you how to use a plugin
to create a great-looking design for your homepage.

At the end of this chapter, your site should look like the image
below. Don't worry if your site isn't an exact match. So long as
your site looks similar and you understand the concepts in this
chapter, you're ready to proceed.

⊙Wordville   Home   News   About   Location   Attractions ⌄   Contact

Search Wordville

Homepage   Search   Q

Recent Posts

WordPress 5.0 is Here!

Wordville Concert in the Park

WordCamp Europe in Belgrade

Join the Annual WordPress Events!

Welcome to Wordville

Recent Comments

steve on Welcome to Wordville

CHAPTER 11.

WORDPRESS PAGE BUILDERS EXPLAINED

In this chapter, we want to fix the problem of the blank homepage.

As we do this, you're going to learn about a type of WordPress plugin called a "Page Builder". These allow you to design page layouts without any coding knowledge at all.

After this chapter, you will be able to:

- Install a page builder plugin.
- Create custom layouts.
- Add content and design to your new homepage.

GETTING STARTED WITH A PAGE BUILDER

We're going to install a page builder plugin called "Beaver Builder".

- Go to "Plugins" and then "Add New".
- Search for "Beaver Builder".
- Click "Install Now" and then "Activate":

WordPress Page Builder – Beaver Builder

Install Now

More Details

The best drag and drop WordPress Page Builder. Easily build beautiful home pages, professional landing pages, and more with Beaver Builder.

By The Beaver Builder Team

★ ★ ★ ★ ★ (256)

400,000+ Active Installations

Last Updated: 4 weeks ago

Untested with your version of WordPress

- You'll see a large screen that introduces Beaver Builder:

- Go to the front of your site and visit the homepage.
- Click the "Beaver Builder" link in the main menu.

- Click "Cancel" and move past the pop-up messages.

- Click on the "+" icon in the top-right corner.

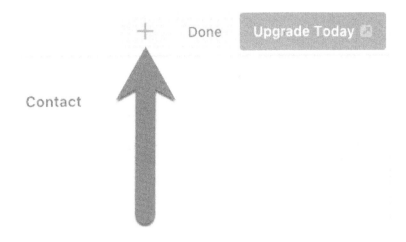

- You'll now see a box with multiple options for redesigning your homepage.

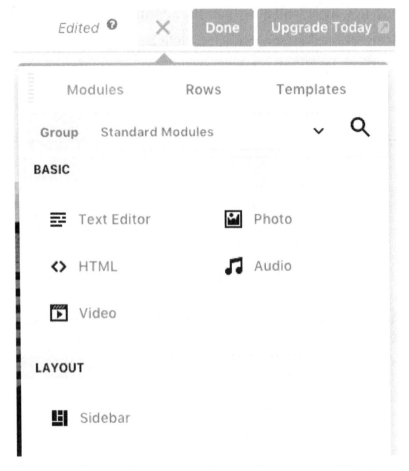

- Let's start by creating a layout for our homepage. Click the "Rows" tab and then select "1 Column".

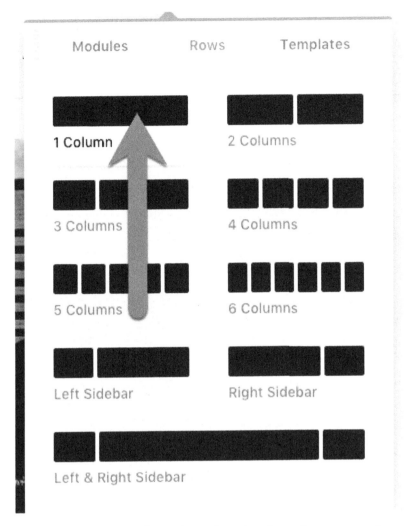

Modules   Rows   Templates

1 Column   2 Columns

3 Columns   4 Columns

5 Columns   6 Columns

Left Sidebar   Right Sidebar

Left & Right Sidebar

- Drag-and-drop the "1 Column" option into the center of your page:

- Repeat that process with "2 Columns". You'll now see a layout with one row on top and two columns underneath:

Now that you have the layout ready, you can place content into these different regions.

- Click the "Modules" link in the top bar.

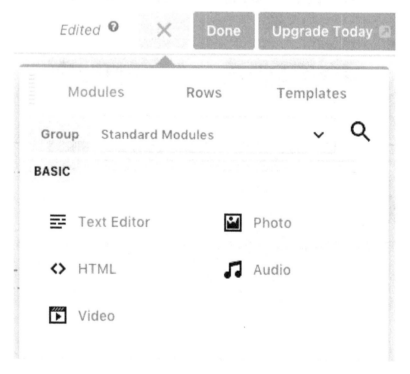

- Select "Photo" and drag it into the top row.

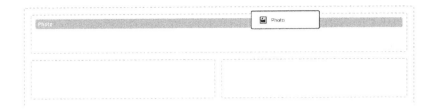

- You will now see a pop-up area on the left-hand side of the page.
- Click the "Select Photo" link.

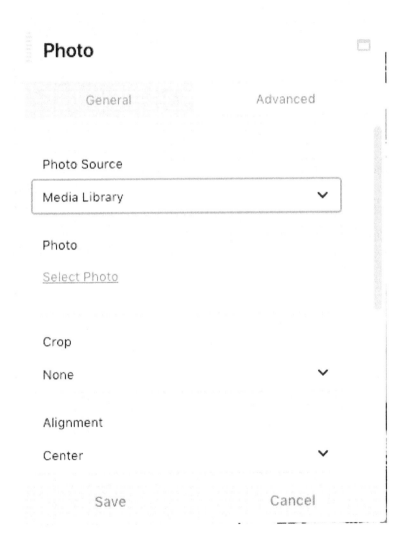

- Choose the wordville-header.png file that you uploaded earlier in the book.

- Click "Save".

- You now see a large header image across the top of your site:

Let's repeat that process to add content for the other parts of our homepage layout:

- Click the "+" icon in the top bar over the site.

- Select "Text Editor".

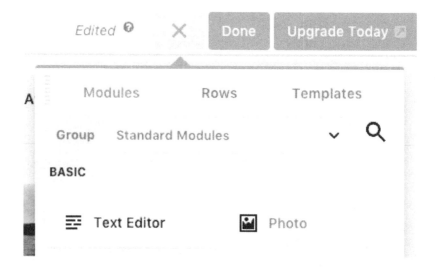

- Drag-and-drop the "Text Editor" box into the bottom-left area of the site.

- You'll see a box with a WordPress Text Editor, as shown in the next image.

- Add some content to welcome people to your site.
- Click "Save".

Let's repeat that process for the other side of our layout.

- Click the "+" icon in the top bar over the site.

- Change the "Group" setting to "WordPress Widgets":

- Look for the "Recent Posts" widget in the right column:

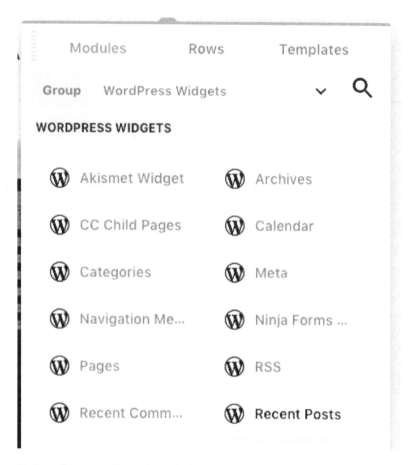

- Select "Recent Posts" and then drag it into the bottom-right column:

- As with the Image and Text Editor, there are some settings you can change. For example, it might be a good idea to improve the Title: "Recent Wordville News":

Widget

General   Advanced

Recent Posts

Title: Recent Wordville News

Number of posts to show: 5

☐ Display post date?

it

Save   Cancel

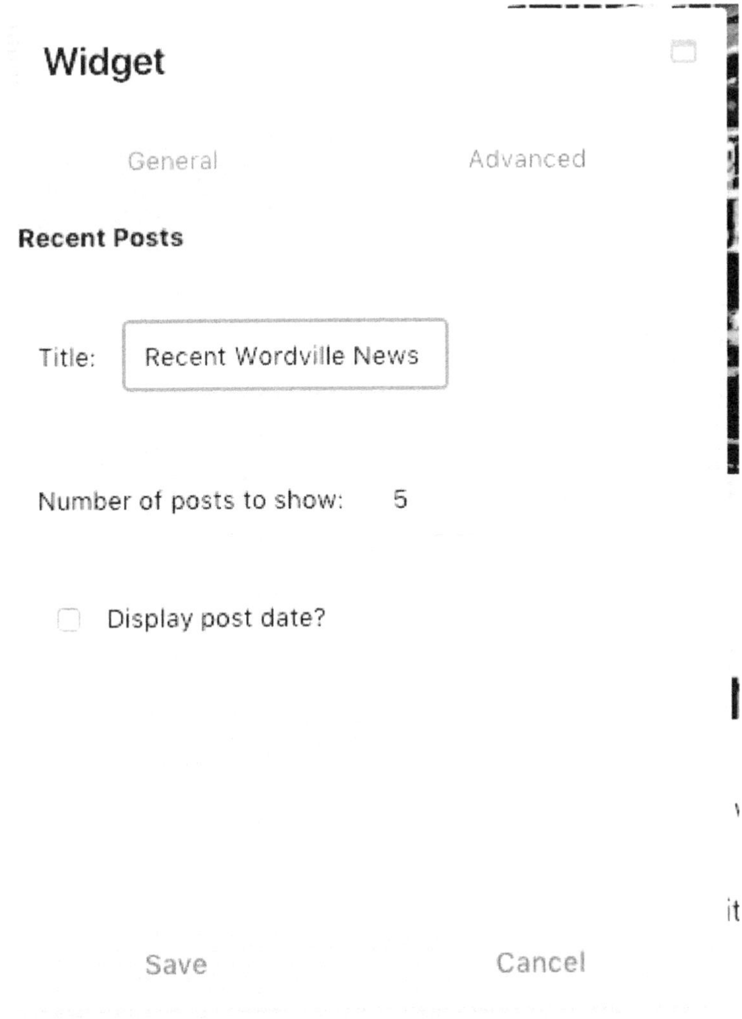

- When you're happy with your changes, click the blue "Done" button in the top-right corner.

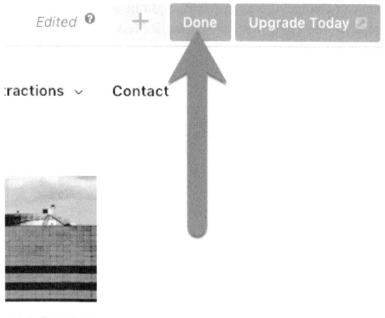

- Click "Publish":

You should now see that you have a good-looking layout for your homepage. Tools such as Beaver Builder can be used for your homepage, but also for other pages as well. They can be really useful ways to quickly build a beautiful site.

Welcome to Wordville

Welcome to the website for the city of Wordville.

This is a community where people love and use WordPress for their websites.

Recent Wordville News

Wordville Concert in the Park
WordCamp Europe in Belgrade
Join the Annual WordPress Events!
Welcome to Wordville

WHAT'S NEXT?

Now that your homepage is complete, we're going to look at another key element that is used to design WordPress sites: widgets.

You've already looked at widgets in several earlier chapters. In the next chapter, we're going to dig into some more advanced widget features.

CHAPTER 12.

WORDPRESS WIDGETS EXPLAINED

You've already dealt with widgets in several different chapters of this book.

Until now, we've placed widgets using the Customizer. In this chapter, we're going to look at the main "Widgets" screen.

After this chapter, you will be able to:

- Understand the main widgets screen.
- Control whether the theme places a sidebar on the page.
- Install a plugin that creates a widget.
- Show different widgets on different pages.

THE WIDGETS SCREEN AND SIDEBARS

The main "Widgets" screen can be found under "Appearance" and then "Widgets".

- On the left side of this screen, we can see all the different kinds of widgets that we could use.
- On the right side of the screen, we have all the different widget areas. The theme controls your widget areas, so these positions are unique to Astra. The image below shows that Astra has eight widget areas.

- Currently, the "Main Sidebar" region contains the most widgets:

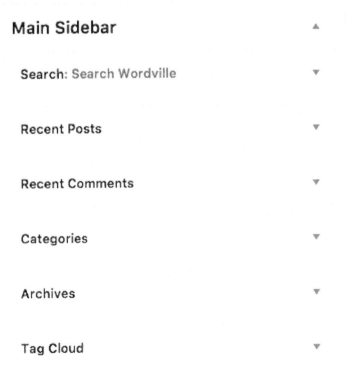

These six widgets appear on the right side of all our blog posts.

So the question arises, why do these widgets appear only on the blog posts? Why do they not appear on the homepage or on pages?

The answer to that is "the theme controls your widgets".

There is a very good reason why the chapter "WordPress Themes Explained" comes before the chapter "WordPress Widgets Explained". Widgets entirely rely on the theme for their placement.

- Go to "Appearance" and then "Customize".
- Click "Layout" and then "Sidebar".

These are the settings that control your theme's sidebars. Here you can move the sidebar to the left or right, or you can hide the sidebar entirely.

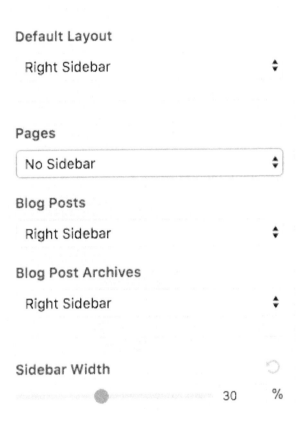

Customizing ▸ Layout

Sidebar

Default Layout

Right Sidebar

Pages

No Sidebar

Blog Posts

Right Sidebar

Blog Post Archives

Right Sidebar

Sidebar Width

30   %

- If you want a sidebar on your pages, choose "Right Sidebar" under the "Pages" dropdown.

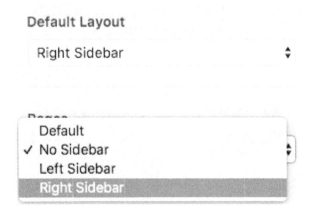

- If you save these theme changes and visit a page on the front of your site, you'll see the sidebar:

ADDING NEW WIDGETS

So we know that the theme controls the widget regions. We can only place a widget in a particular location if the theme allows us to do so.

Widgets are also completely dependent on plugins. If you want to add a new widget, you will need to install a new plugin.

As an example, think about our "Attractions" pages that include "Zoo", "Aquarium", and "Museum". These are connected using the Parent-Child system for pages, but that's not a connection that visitors can see. Let's install a plugin to allow visitors to easily browse through our Attractions.

- Go to "Plugins" and then "Add New".
- Search for the "CC Child Pages" widget.
- Click "Install Now" and then "Activate".

CC Child Pages   Install Now

Adds a responsive shortcode to list child   More Details
and sibling pages. Pre-styled or specify
your own CSS class for custom styling.
Includes child pages widget.

By Caterham Computing

★ ★ ★ ★ ★ (27)   **Last Updated:** 2 weeks ago

6,000+ Active Installations   ✓ **Compatible** with your version of WordPress

- Go to "Appearance" and then "Widgets".
- Move the "CC Child Pages" widget to the "Main Sidebar" region.

Widgets   Manage with Live Preview

Available Widgets   ▲   Main Sidebar   ▲

To activate a widget drag it to a sidebar or click on it. To deactivate a
widget and delete its settings, drag it back.   Search: Search Wordville   ▼

Archives   Audio
                                              Recent Posts   ▼
A monthly archive of your site's   Displays an audio pla
Posts.
                                              Recent Comments   ▼

Calendar   Categ
                                              Categories   ▼
A calendar of your site's Posts.   st or dropdown of categories.

                                              Archives   ▼
CC Child Pages   Custom HTML

Displays current child pages as a   Arbitrary HTML code.   Tag Cloud   ▼
menu

- Set the title for the widget to "Wordville Attractions".
- Check to enable "Show Sibling Pages".

- Click "Save".

Main Sidebar ▲

CC Child Pages: Wordville Attractions ▲

Title:

Wordville Attractions

Show Page Title: ☐
Overrides the Title field, unless parent page has no parent.

Sort by:

Page title ⬍

Exclude:

Page IDs, separated by commas.

Show All Pages: ☐
Overrides the Parent field, shows all top-level pages.

Show Sibling Pages: ☑
Overrides the Parent and Show All field, shows sibling pages.

- Now when you visit the front of your site, go to the "Aquarium" page. In the right sidebar, you'll see links to the other Attractions:

Wordville Attractions

Museum

Zoo

This is great, right?

Not quite. There's still one problem.

This "Wordville Attractions" widget, and all the other widgets, appear on every page, regardless of whether they're needed or not.

DIFFERENT WIDGETS ON DIFFERENT PAGES

A real website needs more flexibility than we've seen so far. You probably do not want to show the same widgets on every single page.

In this part of the chapter, we'll show you how to control which widgets appear on which pages.

- Go to "Plugins" and then "Add New".
- Search for and install the "Widget Options" plugin:

Widget Options

Install Now

Get Better Control over your Widgets. Easily show or hide WordPress widgets on specified pages & devices and/or assign custom alignment.

More Details

By Phpbits Creative Studio

⭐⭐⭐⭐⭐ (704)

30,000+ Active Installations

Last Updated: 5 days ago

✓ **Compatible** with your version of WordPress

- Now when you go to the main "Widgets" screen, look at the active widgets on the right side of the screen. If a widget is placed into a widget area, it will have a variety of options. You can use all sorts of different criteria for hiding the widget.

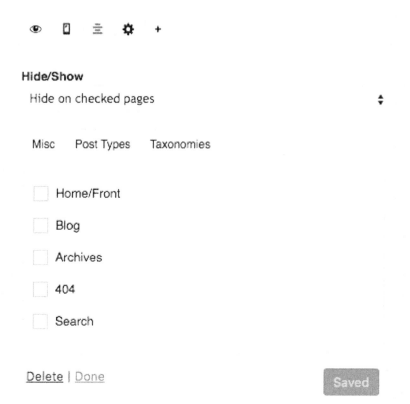

Hide/Show

Hide on checked pages

Misc   Post Types   Taxonomies

☐ Home/Front

☐ Blog

☐ Archives

☐ 404

☐ Search

Delete | Done

Saved

- The choice we want for showing widgets is "Show on checked pages". Select only the three attractions:

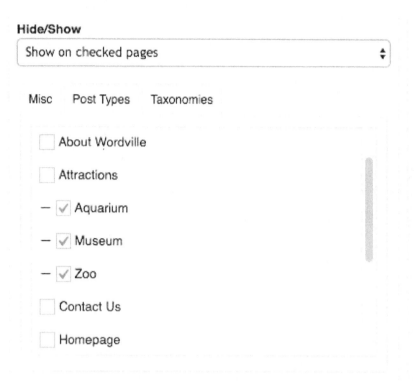

Hide/Show

Show on checked pages

Misc   Post Types   Taxonomies

☐ About Wordville

☐ Attractions

— ☑ Aquarium

— ☑ Museum

— ☑ Zoo

☐ Contact Us

☐ Homepage

Now when you visit your site, the "Wordville Attractions" widget will only appear on the Attractions pages.

WHAT'S NEXT?

In the next chapter, we're going to look at menus.

Menus are another feature that we've looked at in several chapters already. In the chapter "WordPress Menus Explained", we'll dig into some of the more advanced features for your navigation.

CHAPTER 13.

WORDPRESS MENUS EXPLAINED

In this chapter, we are going to talk more about menus and site navigation.

Without good navigation people won't be able to find all the excellent content on your website. I can't stress enough how important quality site navigation is. Good navigation allows visitors to quickly find what they're looking for. Not only do your visitors rely on menus, but Google also reads them. This is one way that Google crawls your website and determines what is important.

After this chapter, you will be able to:

- Understand the Menus screen.
- Create new menus.
- Place menus inside widgets.

THE MENUS SCREEN

Let's take a look at how to make menus in WordPress.

- Navigate to "Appearance" and then "Menus".
- On this screen, you can build your menu by moving links from the left column to the right column:

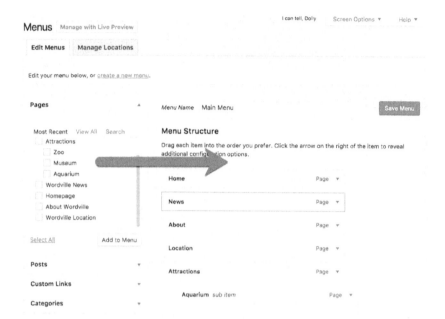

Looking around this screen, you might be asking, "Are these the same features I saw in the Customizer"?

The answer is "yes".

If you click "Manage with Live Preview", you'll be taken to the Customizer; and you can do everything in this chapter from that screen too. My guess is that in a future WordPress version, this "Menus" screen will be removed in favor of the Customizer. The main advantage of this "Menus" screen is that you are using the full screen, which makes it easier to handle larger and more complex menus.

CREATING NEW MENUS

As with widgets, your navigation is entirely dependent on your theme. Your theme is going to provide regions where you can create navigation.

Let's see how that works by creating a new menu.

- Click the "Manage Locations" tab.
- You'll see that the Astra theme has two regions: Primary Menu and Footer Menu.
- Click "Use new menu" next to Footer Menu:

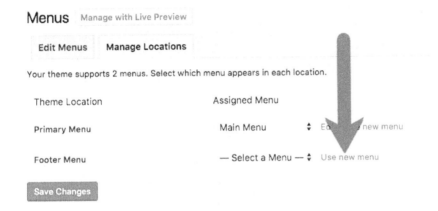

- Menu Name: **Footer Menu**
- Click "Create Menu".

Now you can add links to the menu. Look in the left column, and you can see that you can add "Pages", "Posts", "Custom Links", and "Categories":

In this exercise, we're going to make a menu with useful WordPress-related links. To do that, we need to take advantage of a feature that's currently disabled.

- Open "Screen Options" in the top-right corner.

"Boxes" refers to the options in the left column. For example, if you choose "Submissions", you can link to submissions made through the Ninja Forms plugin. "Show advanced menu properties" allows you to add extra features to your menu.

- Check the box next to "Link Target". This will allow people to visit external links without leaving your site.

- Open the "Custom Links" box.
- URL: **http://wordpress.org**

- Link Text: **WordPress.org**
- Click "Add to Menu".

- In the main part of the screen, open the "WordPress.org" area and check the box that says "Open link in new tab".
- Click the blue "Save Menu" button.

Menu Name   Footer Menu

Menu Structure

Drag each item into the order you prefer. Click the arrow on the right of

WordPress.org   Custom Link   ▲

URL

http://wordpress.org

Navigation Label

WordPress.org

☑ *Open link in a new tab*

Remove | Cancel

Repeat that process for two social accounts for WordPress:

- Open the "Custom Links" box.
- URL: **http://twitter.com/wordpress**
- Link Text: **WordPress on Twitter**
- Click "Add to Menu".
- Check the box that says "Open link in new tab".

And repeat the process for one more link:

- URL: **http://facebook.com/wordpress**
- Link Text: **WordPress on Facebook**

After finishing, your menu structure will look like the image below. Make sure you click "Save Menu" before moving on.

Menu Name   Footer Menu

Menu Structure

Drag each item into the order you prefer. Click the arrow on the right (

WordPress.org   Custom Link   ▼

WordPress on Twitter   Custom Link   ▼

WordPress on Facebook   Custom Link   ▼

Now we publish the menu. We need to rely on the theme for this:

- Go to "Appearance" and then "Customize".
- Click "Layout" -> "Footer" -> "Footer Bar".

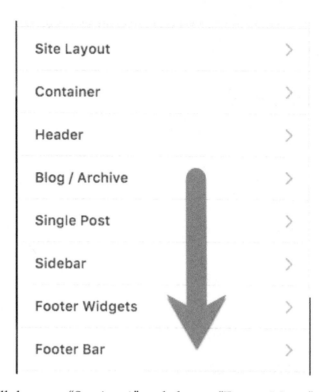

- Scroll down to "Section 1" and choose "Footer Menu":

Section 1

Custom Text   ⬍

Section 1 Custom Text

Copyright © [current ar] [site_title]

Section 2

✓ None
Footer Menu
Custom Text
Widget

- You should now be able to see your footer menu on the site, although the links won't be active until you click "Publish" and visit the front of the site.

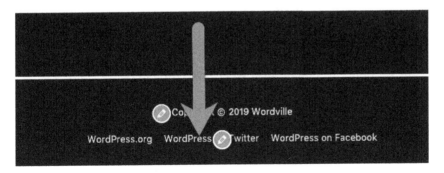

PLACING MENUS INSIDE WIDGETS

As we've seen in this chapter, your theme has pre-defined positions for menus.

However, you can also use menus in other areas. For example, you can use menus inside widgets. This will give you more flexibility, because most themes have many widget positions. For example, the Astra theme has two pre-defined menu positions, but it has eight widget areas.

- Go to "Appearance" then "Widgets".
- Choose the "Navigation Menu" widget.
- Drag this widget into the "Main Sidebar" area.
- Title: **Key Wordville Links**
- Select Menu: **Footer Menu**

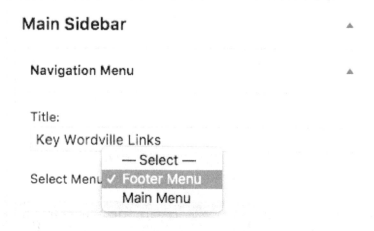

Now if you visit the front of your site, you can see this menu appearing on any page with the Main Sidebar:

Key Wordville Links

WordPress.org

WordPress on Twitter

WordPress on Facebook

WHAT'S NEXT?

Over the last few chapters we've talked a lot about the design and layout of your WordPress site. We've covered themes, page builders, widgets, and menus.

Your site now looks like a complete WordPress site. It should look similar to the image below. As always, don't worry about matching my image exactly. So long as you understand the concepts in the last few chapters, you're ready to continue.

You've built your site, so now it's time to welcome your users. In the next chapter, we're going to talk about user permissions and what your visitors can and cannot do on your site.

Wordville

Welcome to Wordville

Welcome to the website for the city of Wordville.

This is community where people love and use WordPress for their websites.

Recent Wordville News

Wordville Concert in the Park

WordCamp Europe in Belgrade

Join the Annual WordPress Events!

Welcome to Wordville

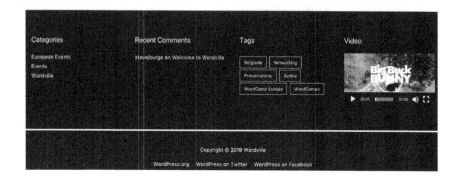

CHAPTER 14.

WORDPRESS USERS EXPLAINED

In this chapter, we are going to talk about how to manage users in WordPress.

If you are only running a blog for yourself and you are the only user, then you don't really need to worry about it too much as you wouldn't have any other users. We will take a look at how to manage users and the different possible roles they may have.

After this chapter, you will be able to:

- Understand the "Users" screen.
- Understand roles in WordPress.
- Test different roles.
- Customize roles.

THE USERS SCREEN

In the admin area, under the "Users" link, you can view all the users on your site. Right now, you only have one user, and it's you.

When you are looking at the Users screen in the admin area, you can see how many posts a person has written, their role, their email address and their name. You will also see a photo, which is called a Gravatar. The Gravatar is associated with http://gravatar.com, and it is used only if the user has an account with Gravatar using the same email address as on your WordPress site.

From here you can edit users, delete users, or search for them using the search box. On a site with many users, the search functionality can be very useful.

It's also possible to change the permissions given to each user. You haven't really seen this feature yet. This is because you can only change the role for others, even if you are an Administrator. Let's take a look at roles and permissions.

- Click "Add new".

- Create a new account using either dummy information or another email address that you own. You can always use "example.com" because that has been set aside specifically for situations like this.

Add New User

Create a brand new user and add them to this site.

Username *(required)*	testuser
Email *(required)*	testuser@example.com
First Name	testuser
Last Name	testuser

- WordPress will create a strong password for you.
- The default screen does not show the password. Click "Show password".

Password	vLnjr%a9Low2B8TGS6SdmhfF	🚫 Hide Cancel
	Strong	

- If you want to choose a simpler password that's easy to guess, WordPress will force you to acknowledge that your password is weak:

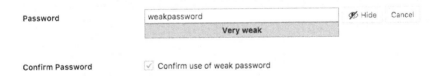

Password	weakpassword	🚫 Hide Cancel
	Very weak	
Confirm Password	☑ Confirm use of weak password	

- At the bottom of the page, you will see the "Role" area. This is the most important part of this chapter.
- Choose "Subscriber" and then click "Add new User":

Role

- You'll now have two users on your site:

Username	Name	Email	Role	Posts
steve@ostraining.com	Steve Burge	steve@ostraining.com	Administrator	5
testuser	testuser testuser	testuser@example.com	Subscriber	0
Username	Name	Email	Role	Posts

UNDERSTANDING THE USER ROLES

There are five roles available for WordPress users: Subscriber, Contributor, Author, Editor, Administrator.

A Subscriber can do very little on your site. There is very little they can do besides change their own name and their own password. What they can do is log into the front-end of your site and post comments without waiting for an Administrator to approve them.

A Contributor is the next level up and has more permissions than a Subscriber. A Contributor can log into the WordPress dashboard. This image shows what they will see.

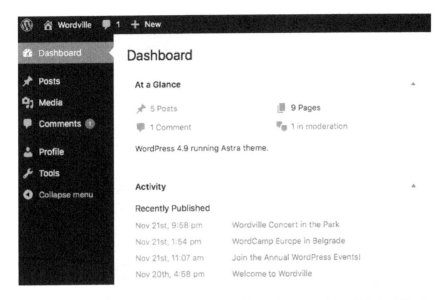

A Contributor can write content, but they can't publish. Their posts must be reviewed by the Editor or the Administrator. When a Contributor writes a post, they won't be able to publish their post. They will only see "Submit for Review".

The next step up from Contributor is Author.

An Author can do anything with their own content. This means they can write, edit, publish and unpublish, but only on their own content. If the Author goes to the "Posts" screen, they won't be able to access anyone else's content. Other content will be grayed-out with no "Edit" link available.

	Title	Author	Categories
☐	WordCamp Europe in Belgrade View	Steve Burge	European Events, Events
	Wordville Concert in the Park	Steve Burge	Wordville

An Editor can make any changes to anyone's content. However, they cannot change plugins, themes or settings. The image below shows what an Editor sees when they log in:

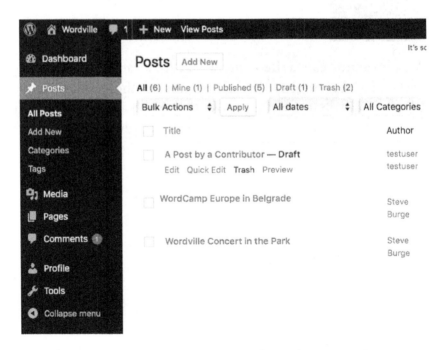

An Administrator is the most powerful role in WordPress. An Administrator has full power to do everything. They can manage themes, content, plugins, users and everything else. You have been an Administrator throughout this book.

This chart gives you a handy overview of what users can and cannot do:

	Subscriber	Contributor	Author	Editor	Administrator
Log in to the WordPress admin area	✓	✓	✓	✓	✓
Read posts	✓	✓	✓	✓	✓
Comment on posts	✓	✓	✓	✓	✓
Edit and delete own unpublished posts		✓	✓	✓	✓
Edit and delete own published posts			✓	✓	✓
Publish own posts			✓	✓	✓
Upload files to media library			✓	✓	✓
Publish, edit and delete any post or page				✓	✓
Manage categories				✓	✓
Moderate comments				✓	✓
Manage plugins and widgets					✓
Add or remove users					✓
Edit themes					✓

TESTING THE USER ROLES

The best way to learn about the five user roles in WordPress is to test them.

- Go to "Plugins" and then "Add New".
- Search for, install and activate the "User Switching" plugin:

User Switching   Install Now

Instant switching between user   More Details
accounts in WordPress.

By John Blackbourn

★ ★ ★ ★ ★ (139)   Last Updated: 2 weeks ago

80,000+ Active Installations   ✓ Compatible with your version of WordPress

- Go to the "Users" page.
- Hover over the testuser account, and click the "Switch To" link that appears.

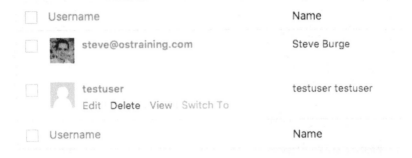

- You'll now see your WordPress site through the eyes of a "Subscriber". They really can't do anything!

- Have a browse around the site, and then click the "Switch back to" link.

- Now that you are an Administrator again, go to the "Users" screen.

- Click "Edit" for the "testuser" account.

- Change the "testuser" account to "Contributor".

- Scroll to the bottom of the screen and click "Update User".

- Click "Switch To" and test the permissions as a Contributor.

- Repeat this process for the Author, Editor, and Administrator roles.

When you promote the "testuser" to be an Administrator, you'll find that they really can do everything on your site. They can even delete your main Administrator account. Please don't do this, and please be careful who you give the "Administrator" role to. Administrators really can control every aspect of your website.

CUSTOMIZE USER ROLES

WordPress arrives with five user roles, but these can be changed and expanded. Using a plugin called "Members", I'm going to show you how to customize the roles on your site.

- Go to "Plugins" and then "Add New".
- Search for, install, and activate the Members plugin:

Members

The most powerful user, role, and capability management plugin for WordPress.

By Justin Tadlock

Install Now

More Details

★ ★ ★ ★ ★ (198)

100,000+ Active Installations

Last Updated: 3 weeks ago

Untested with your version of WordPress

- Now under the "Users" menu link, you will see more options. "Roles" and "Add New Role" are now options.

In this exercise, imagine that you're working with a developer to build your site. You want to give them almost all the permissions of an Administrator, but you're not comfortable allowing them to delete your account!

- Go to "Roles" and then click "Clone" under "Administrator":

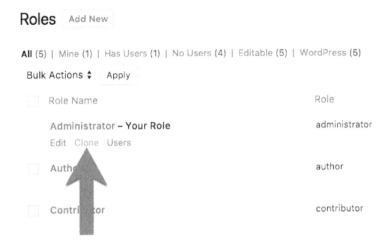

- Change the name of the role to "Developer":

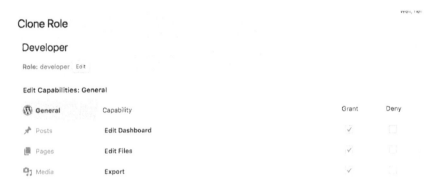

You'll see that every role in WordPress has a checkbox for "Grant" or "Deny". We want to stop the Developer from deleting users.

- Click "Users" in the left column, between "Plugins" and "Custom" (this is different from the "Users" link in the normal, black WordPress admin menu).

- Choose "Deny" for the "Delete Roles" and "Delete Users" options.

- Click "Add Role" to finish.

Edit Capabilities: Users

General	Capability		Grant	Deny
Posts	Create Roles		✓	☐
Pages	Create Users		✓	☐
Media	Delete Roles		☐	✓
Submissions	Delete Users		☐	✓
Taxonomies	Edit Roles		✓	☐
Appearance	Edit Users		☐	✓
Plugins	List Roles		✓	☐
Users	List Users		✓	☐
Custom	Promote Users		☐	✓
All	Remove Users		☐	✓
	Capability		Grant	Deny

You can now test the new user role.

- Go to "Users" and change the "testuser" account to be a Developer.

- Click "Switch To" and try out your new user role.

- Browse to the "Users" page, and you will not be able to delete your main account. Even if you disable the Members plugin, you still won't be able to evade this restriction.

Username	Name	Email
steve@ostraining.com View Switch To	Steve Burge	steve@ostraining.com
testuser	testuser testuser	testuser@example.com
Username	Name	Email

NEW USER ROLES AND PLUGINS

When you install a plugin, they often create new user roles.

This is very common with e-commerce plugins. When you install popular plugins, such as WooCommerce, you may end up with roles such as "Inventory Manager" or "Sales Manager". These roles allow someone to log in and deal only with e-commerce materials and never see any WordPress content or settings.

If you install a photography plugin, you might end up with a variety of roles that restrict users to uploading and managing photos.

If you install a project management plugin, you may end with roles for the Project Manager and roles for the customer.

WHAT'S NEXT?

In the next chapter, we're going to wrap up our site and see whether it's ready to take live.

Throughout this book, you've learned a wide variety of new WordPress skills. Has that been enough to build a complete WordPress site?

CHAPTER 15.

FINISHING AND LAUNCHING YOUR SITE

As you have gone through this book, you've been building a site called Wordville.

At this point in your site-building process, it's time to take a careful look over everything you've built. Is it ready for launch, or do you need to make further changes?

The image below shows how your WordPress site may appear at this point. Don't worry if your site doesn't match this image 100%. In fact, I'd like to think you had some ideas and inspiration of your own and are starting to feel comfortable about making your own site changes.

This homepage was built using the Beaver Builder page builder plugin. You have a large image on the top row. In the second row, you have a text box saying "Welcome to Wordville" and a widget with a list of recent Wordville news.

Home   News   About   Location   Attractions ⌄   Contact

Welcome to Wordville

Welcome to the website for the city of Wordville.

This is community where people love and use WordPress for their websites

Recent Wordville News

Wordville Concert in the Park

WordCamp Europe in Belgrade

Join the Annual WordPress Events!

Welcome to Wordville

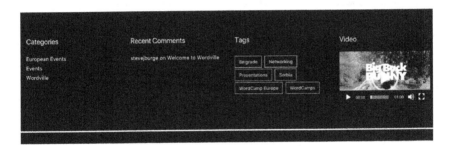

- Click on the "News" menu link, and you'll see a very different page. This page is almost entirely built with core WordPress features. This is a standard blog layout that was originally on our homepage. We moved it to an inside page using the options available in "Settings" and then "Reading". On the right side of the screen are a series of WordPress widgets.

Wordville

Home   News   About   Location   Attractions ⌄   Contact

Key Wordville Links

WordPress.org
WordPress on Twitter
WordPress on Facebook

Search Wordville

Search...   Q

Recent Posts

WordPress 5.0 is Here!
Wordville Concert in the Park
WordCamp Europe in Belgrade
Join the Annual WordPress Events!
Welcome to Wordville

Recent Comments

Join the Annual WordPress Events! –
Wordville on Welcome to Wordville

WordPress 5.0 is Here!

Leave a Comment / Wordville / By Steve Burge

The WordPress team have just released the latest WordPress update.

- Click through to "Attractions" and then "Aquarium", and you'll be navigating through a dropdown menu that you created using the drag-and-drop feature for menu links. On the page, you'll see a photo gallery that was created without using any extra plugins.

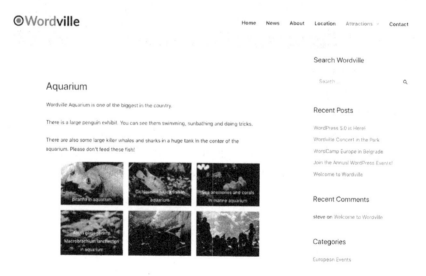

Wordville

Home   News   About   Location   Attractions ⌄   Contact

Search Wordville

Search...   Q

Aquarium

Wordville Aquarium is one of the biggest in the country.

There is a large penguin exhibit. You can see them swimming, sunbathing and doing tricks.

There are also some large killer whales and sharks in a huge tank in the center of the aquarium. Please don't feed these fish!

Recent Posts

WordPress 5.0 is Here!
Wordville Concert in the Park
WordCamp Europe in Belgrade
Join the Annual WordPress Events!
Welcome to Wordville

Recent Comments

steve on Welcome to Wordville

Categories

European Events

- Click "Contact" and you'll see a contact form that was created with the Ninja Forms plugin. By default, WordPress doesn't have a contact form of any kind, let alone one that can use a variety of custom fields and then store the submissions successfully in the database.

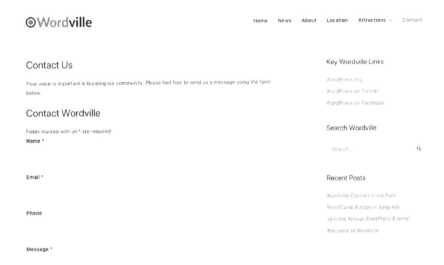

WHAT'S NEXT?

Now our website, Wordville, looks like a real city site. We have photos, attractions, contact information, news, and much more.

You've reached Step 6 in the WordPress workflow: Launch.

However, finishing your site is not the end of the WordPress workflow. Owning a website is a lot like owning a pet or a plant in that it requires constant care. Once we've launched our site, we need to keep it safe, updated and running quickly.

In the final chapter, we're going to introduce you to Step 7, where you'll learn how to manage your WordPress site. You're going to see how to maintain, update and back up your site. You'll also learn how to guard against comment spam and use a staging site.

Each of these topics are things that you will use in your day-to-day maintenance of your WordPress site.

1. **Planning**

2. **Content**

3. **Plugins**

4. **Design**

5. **Users**

6. **Launch**

7. **Maintenance**

CHAPTER 16.

WORDPRESS SITE MAINTENANCE EXPLAINED

In this final chapter, we're going to turn our attention to keeping your WordPress site safe, secure and running quickly.

Throughout this book, you've built your WordPress site.

However, it's not enough to just build a great site. You need to look after it and maintain it. That's going to be our focus in this chapter. How do you ensure your site is successful over the long term?

After this chapter, you will be able to:

- Keep your site safe.
- Update your site.
- Backup your site.
- Choose a security plugin.
- Fight spam comments.
- Speed up your site.

KEEPING YOUR WORDPRESS SITE SAFE

To kick off this chapter, we're going to take a look at security in WordPress.

WordPress is really safe and secure software. There have been very few serious security problems with WordPress over the years.

Anytime you read an article about how insecure WordPress is, it's almost always talking about plugins and themes written by third parties who may not be the most security-conscious. With over 50,000 plugins in the WordPress plugin directory, it's inevitable that some plugins will have issues.

Absolutely the best thing you can do for your WordPress site is to keep your site up-to-date. If your WordPress site is up-to-date, including the plugins and themes you installed, then your site is highly likely to be secure.

UPDATING YOUR WORDPRESS SITE

How do you know which version of WordPress you need?

That's easy. There is only ever one acceptable version of WordPress, and that's the latest version. Other software may have multiple versions at the same time. WordPress only ever has one version.

- In your WordPress site, click "Updates":

Does your site say, "You have the latest version of WordPress."?

WordPress Updates

Last checked on February 3, 2019 at 8:06 pm.   Check Again

You have the latest version of WordPress. Future security updates will be applied automatically.

If you need to re-install version 5.0.3, you can do so here:

Re-install Now

Plugins

Your plugins are all up to date.

Themes

Your themes are all up to date.

If you are not running the latest version of WordPress, you'll see several nagging messages inside your site:

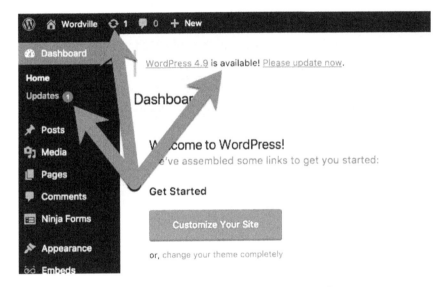

- Click one of the notices you see in the image above.

- Click the blue "Update Now" button. That's all you need to do – WordPress will then complete the site update for you.

WordPress Updates

Important: before updating, please back up your database and files. For help with updates, visit the Updating WordPress Codex page.

Last checked on November 24, 2017 at 2:45 pm.   Check Again

An updated version of WordPress is available.

You can update to WordPress 4.9 automatically:

Update Now

While your site is being updated, it will be in maintenance mode. As soon as your updates are complete, your site will return to normal.

Fortunately, if you're forgetful or don't log into your site very often, WordPress does have automatic updates for security issues. So if somebody finds a security flaw in WordPress, it gets patched and your site gets automatically updated without you even having to do anything.

WordPress has major versions such as 4.7, 4.8, 4.9 and 5.0. These versions will not update automatically. A security release will have a number with three digits such as 4.8.1 or 4.8.2. WordPress will simply recognize that there is an update, get the new version and and install it for you. Your site will email you when that occurs. It's possible to turn this functionality off if you don't need it, but I don't recommend it.

In addition to updating the WordPress core, you should absolutely keep your themes and plugins up-to-date.

- Updates for your themes and plugins will also appear in the "Updates" area of your WordPress site. In the image below, my copy of Ninja Forms needs to be updated:

Plugins

The following plugins have new versions available. Check the ones you want to update and then click "Update Plugins".

Update Plugins

☐ Select All

☐ **Ninja Forms**
You have version 3.2.3 installed. Update to 3.2.4. View version 3.2.4 details.
Compatibility with WordPress 4.9: Unknown

☐ Select All

If you're not using a plugin, I highly recommend removing it from your site.

- A plugin can't be deleted while it's active, so the first step to remove a plugin is to click "Deactivate":

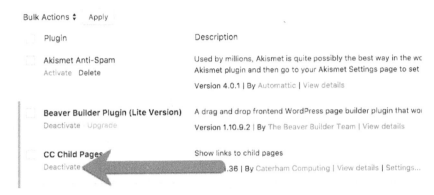

- Once you've deactivated a plugin, you can then click "Delete":

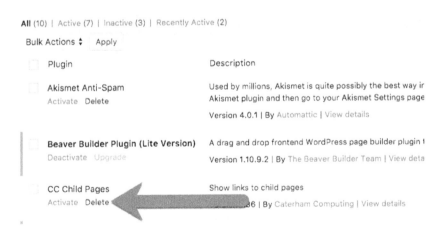

If you have a lot of sites to maintain, it's worth looking at service such as http://managewp.com. ManageWP provides a single dashboard where you can update all your sites with a single click. They also have advanced features, such as creating a backup of your site every time you run an update.

CHOOSING A SECURITY PLUGIN

Once you feel comfortable keeping your WordPress site up-to-date, there are some plugins that you can install to help prevent certain kinds of attacks.

One very popular plugin is called iThemes Security.

iThemes Security has several useful security features.

One iThemes Security feature is called "Brute Force Protection". A brute force attack means that somebody is trying to log into your website over and over again by using a computer to do the logging in, which means they can do it many times per second.

They may never actually break in, but the mere fact that they are trying to over-and-over again can slow your server down and make your site seem slow. "Brute Force Protection" helps stop that. After a certain amount of unsuccessful login attempts, the person who is trying to log in gets blacklisted and they can't attempt to log in anymore.

After installing iThemes Security, the plugin offers to configure itself for you. Click "Secure Site" and it will provide a useful default configuration:

Security Check

Some features and settings are recommended for every site to run. This tool will ensure that your site is using these recommendations.

When the button below is clicked the following modules will be enabled and configured:

- Banned Users
- Database Backups
- Local Brute Force Protection
- Network Brute Force Protection
- Strong Passwords
- WordPress Tweaks

Secure Site

Another plugin I want to draw your attention to is from http://sucuri.net. Sucuri does a variety of things, including cleaning up after you've been hacked. This plugin that they offer is for scanning. It can scan your website looking for malicious software to find out if you've already been hacked. It can also make recommendations on things that you can do to prevent being hacked. It looks at your settings and configurations and suggests changes to make. It also checks search engines to see if your site has been blacklisted for malware and makes you aware of it before your users know. All-in-all, Sucuri offers an excellent service, and we use them to protect our sites.

Sucuri Security – Auditing, Malware Scanner and Security Hardening

Install Now

More Details

The Sucuri WordPress Security plugin is a security toolset for security integrity monitoring, malware detection and security hardening.

By Sucuri Inc.

 (285)

Last Updated: 3 months ago

300,000+ Active Installations

Untested with your version of WordPress

BACKING UP YOUR WORDPRESS SITE

Regular backups may seem like a tedious chore, but I promise you that the day your site goes down and it seems to be gone forever, you will be happy you have a backup.

The first place to go for backups is your hosting company. Any company worth using will provide you with a backup service.

It's also worth considering your own system of backups so you don't rely 100% on your hosting company.

One good backup plugin is called BackWPup.

BackWPup – WordPress Backup Plugin

Install Now

Schedule complete automatic backups of your WordPress installation. Decide which content will be stored (Dropbox, S3...). This is the free version

More Details

By Inpsyde GmbH

(571)

Last Updated: 4 days ago

600,000+ Active Installations

✓ Compatible with your version of WordPress

- Install and activate BackWPUp.

- Go to "BackWPUp" and then "Jobs".
- Click "Add new".
- Please name this job: **Nightly Backup**

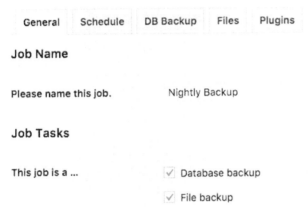

The most important part of this process is under "Job Destination". To be valuable as a backup, you need to send your backup to a different destination. If you have a problem with your server, and your backups are stored on your server, then your backups aren't going to be very helpful!

If you have an account with any of these services, I would highly recommend sending your backups to one of them.

Where should your backup file be stored?

- [ ] Backup to Folder
- [ ] Backup sent via email
- [ ] Backup to FTP
- [ ] Backup to Dropbox
- [ ] Backup to an S3 Service
- [ ] Backup to Microsoft Azure (Blob)
- [ ] Backup to Rackspace Cloud Files
- [ ] Backup to SugarSync

For example, if you choose "Backup to an S3 Service" and click "Save changes", you'll see a new tab. Here you can enter your Amazon S3 login details:

General	Schedule	DB Backup	Files	Plugins	To: S3 Service

S3 Service

Select a S3 service   Amazon S3: US Standard   ‡

Or a S3 Server URL

S3 Access Keys

Access Key

Secret Key

- After saving the settings on the first screen, click the "Schedule" tab. Choosing "with WordPress cron" is the easy option.

BackWPup › Job: Nightly Backup

| General | Schedule | DB Backup | Files | Plugins | To: S3 Service |

Job Schedule

Start job   ◯ manually only

                ◉ with WordPress cron

                with EasyCron.com - *First setup API Key.*

- At the bottom of the screen, you can also choose how often this backup is made. The default choice is daily at 3 am in the morning.

Scheduler

Type		Hour	Minute
◯ monthly	on 1 ⬍	3 ⬍	0 ⬍
◯ weekly	Sunday ⬍	3 ⬍	0 ⬍
◉ daily		3 ⬍	0 ⬍
◯ hourly			0 ⬍

- Now you have a nightly backup job. You can test whether it works by clicking "Run now".

FIGHTING SPAM

In this part of the chapter, we are going to talk about how to fight comment spam. If you have comments turned on anywhere on your site – even if it's just one post from a long time ago – you will get spam.

If you don't want comments on your site, I'd highly recommend turning them off using a plugin such as Disable Comments:

Disable Comments

Allows administrators to globally disable comments on their site. Comments can be disabled according to post type. Multisite friendly.

By Samir Shah

Install Now

More Details

⭐⭐⭐⭐⭐ (199)

1+ Million Active Installations

Last Updated: 6 days ago

✓ **Compatible** with your version of WordPress

If you want comments on your site, then you will need to deal with spam. WordPress has a built-in ability to mark a comment as spam. In the "Comments" screen, click the "Spam" link as shown below:

Comments

All (2) | Pending (0) | Approved (2) | Spam (0) | Trash (0)

Bulk Actions ⬍ Apply All comment types ⬍ Filter

Author	Comment
Join the Annual WordPress Events! – Wordville wpexplained.com/2017/11/21/join-the-annual-wordpr... 127.0.0.1	[...] Are you new to WordPress? Click here to find out more. [...]
stevejburge steve@ostraining.com 127.0.0.1	WordPress seems super-exciting. Thanks for this info! Unapprove Reply Quick Edit Edit Spam Trash
Author	Comment

You can go mark these comments as spam, and then they would end up in the spam folder. Unfortunately moving a comment to the spam folder doesn't really do anything beyond remove it from the view of visitors.

What you really want is a system that can read your comments for you, figure out which ones are spam, and then deal with them appropriately.

If you go to http://wordpress.org/plugins and search for the term "spam", you will note that there are more than a thousand different plugins for dealing with spam. When choosing an anti-spam plugin, use the same methods that we spoke about when choosing any other plugin. Look for active installs, recent updates, how old it is, and how many stars it has.

One plugin that I want to point out is called Akismet. A copy of Akismet comes with every install of WordPress.

Akismet has been around since 2005 and has an enormous database of spam, which helps it accurately decide what is spam and what is not. However, if a spam comment gets through, Akismet lets you report it, which increases their future accuracy.

I want to point out that Akismet requires an API key. For the basic features, you can choose the "Name Your Price" option and your account will be free.

CHAPTER 17.

WHAT'S NEXT?

Congratulations! You've reached the end of the main portion of WordPress Explained!

Throughout the book, each chapter has followed on logically from the next. We've aimed to teach you WordPress using the 7-step workflow shown below.

Why do we recommend following this workflow?

First. WordPress has a lot of moving pieces, and it's very helpful to follow a consistent approach.

Second, many of the problems we hear from users are caused by not following this workflow:

- Some users will skip Step #1 and end up with a messy, unplanned site.
- Some users jump directly to Step #6 and try to fix their site's problems in full view of their visitors.
- Some users skip Step #7 and find that their site is out-of-date and insecure.

If you follow these 7 steps in this order, you will end up with a successful WordPress site.

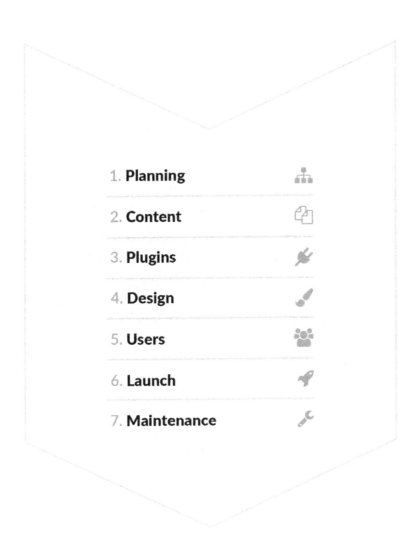

1. Planning	
2. Content	
3. Plugins	
4. Design	
5. Users	
6. Launch	
7. Maintenance	

ARE YOU STUCK ON A WORDPRESS PROBLEM?

One of the great things about WordPress being so popular is that almost every problem you run into has been encountered by other people. Many of those people will have asked for or posted a solution to their problem online.

If you ever get stuck, here are the first two places you should go to for help:

- **Contact us**: Get in touch by emailing books@ostraining.com.

- **Use Google**: If you get an error message or encounter a problem, type it directly into a search engine, and there's a good chance you'll find a solution.

- **Use the WordPress help forums**: https://wordpress.org/support/. The WordPress forums have millions of posts, so you can find a lot of solutions. Search for a solution to your question, and if you don't find it, write a new post. There's sure to be someone who can help you.

- **Join the WordPress community**: WordPress doesn't rely on money; it relies on people like you. Whether you attend a local WordPress event, post solutions you find on the forum, or even say thank you to someone who's helped you, there are many easy ways to become part of the WordPress community. The more you rely on WordPress for your website or your business, the more it can benefit you to become part of the community.

We hope to see you around in the WordPress community, and we wish you all the best in your use of WordPress!

WHAT SHOULD YOU DO NEXT?

- **Practice**. The only way to get better at WordPress is to build WordPress sites. Decide on your first WordPress project and start practicing.

- **Practice now**. You will forget most of what you've read in this book. That's human nature and doesn't make us bad teachers or you a bad learner. The longer you wait to practice WordPress, the more you'll forget. Why not start right away?

- **Learn more**. We guarantee that there are things you will come across while using WordPress that haven't been included in this book. This book has only a limited number of pages, and we've tried to focus on only the most important things about WordPress. We also tried hard to avoid any code so that the barrier to entry for using WordPress is as low as possible. However, we do have some bonus chapters for you!

BONUS CHAPTERS IN THIS BOOK

Yes, the main part of the book has finished, but as an extra treat we've included some bonus chapters.

Why did we not include these chapters in the main part of the book?

- These are topics that are very helpful to know about, but not every WordPress user needs to know.

- Rather than following through in a step-by-step order, you can read each of these chapters individually.

The next two chapters cover optimizing your WordPress site and WordPress eCommerce. If any of those topics interest you, turn to the appropriate page and let's learn some more WordPress!

CHAPTER 18.

BONUS: OPTIMIZING WORDPRESS EXPLAINED

In this bonus chapter, we're going to take a look at a few ways to optimize and improve your WordPress site.

First, we'll look at ways to improve your search engine rankings.

Second, we'll see how to make your site run as quickly as possible.

Finally, we'll show you how to plan and publish high-quality content.

HOW TO OPTIMIZE WORDPRESS FOR SEARCH ENGINES

In the early part of this book, we talked about technical improvements to your website.

But, if you can't write content that visitors and search engines find interesting, then all the optimizations in the world won't help you.

Let's take a look at how you can write content that is SEO optimized. This applies to your WooCommerce product pages, plus also blog posts and other content on your site. The most popular solution in the WordPress world for that is Yoast SEO (https://yoast.com). They have a free plugin on WordPress.org that helps you write optimized content.

Yoast SEO

Improve your WordPress SEO: Write better content and have a fully optimized WordPress site using the Yoast SEO plugin.

By Team Yoast

Install Now

More Details

⭐⭐⭐⭐⭐ (18,648)

1+ Million Active Installations

Last Updated: 2 weeks ago

✔ **Compatible** with your version of WordPress

The Yoast plugin provides tools and advice that help you write optimized product descriptions. It will remind you to use your SEO keyword in your title and text, add alt tags to images, link to other pages in your site, and a lot of other SEO best practices.

- Install the Yoast SEO plugin.
- Go to "Posts" and edit your "Welcome to Wordville" post.
- Scroll down and look for the "Yoast SEO" box under the main text area.

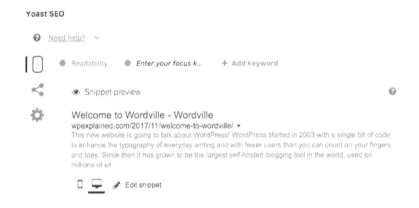

Your first task is to choose a "Focus keyword" at the bottom of this box. This is the single keyword that you are optimizing your product for. The normal advice of SEO experts is that your pages should focus on a single phrase. If you try and rank your site for many different keywords and key phrases, the page will not be focused enough to rank well.

- In this example, let's choose "wordville" as our keyword. Enter that into the "Focus keyword" box.
- Click "Update" in the "Publish" box in the top-right corner of the post editing screen.

🔍 Focus keyword   ❓

wordville

☐ This article is cornerstone content

After you enter a Focus keyword, look at the "Publish" box. Here you can see a "Readability" score and an "SEO" score. Both of these boxes are currently yellow, which means we have work to do. Yoast SEO works on a traffic-light system: green is good, and red is bad.

Publish ▲

Preview Changes

📍 Status: **Published** Edit

👁 Visibility: **Public** Edit

🕐 Revisions: **6** Browse

📅 Published on: **Nov 20, 2017 @ 16:58**
Edit

Publicize: Not Connected
Show

ʏ Readability: **OK**

ʏ SEO: **OK**

Move to Trash   Update

- Scroll back down to the "Yoast SEO" box, and you'll see recommendations for improving your product content. As you fix each of these issues, the red marks will turn green.

≣ Analysis

⌃ Problems (4)

● The focus keyword doesn't appear in the first paragraph of the copy. Make sure the topic is clear immediately.

● The keyword density is 0%, which is too low; the focus keyword was found 0 times.

● No meta description has been specified. Search engines will display copy from the page instead.

● No internal links appear in this page, consider adding some as appropriate.

⌄ Improvements (5)

⌄ Good results (4)

When you've finished implementing the advice from Yoast SEO, the "Publish" box will show two green check marks:

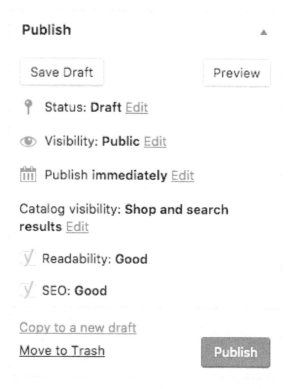

Yoast SEO makes it easy to find which of your posts need optimization. If you look at the main "Posts" screen, you'll see a new filter: "All SEO Scores". This filter allows you to find only the posts that are marked as "Needs Improvement" or simply, "OK". You can also visually see the posts' scores in the right-hand column using the red / yellow / green system.

HOW TO SPEED UP YOUR WORDPRESS SITE

Making your site load fast is a big topic, and you'll hear people suggest many different solutions.

First and foremost, you want to make sure you use a good host. An excellent host will put you on a fast server. The difference between a bad hosting company and a good hosting company can be a 300% or 400% speed boost. Nothing will speed up your site effectively if you have poor-quality hosting.

Some hosting companies, and some WordPress users, will advise you to use a caching plugin. Some of these plugins are very popular indeed. The most popular of all is WP Super Cache with over 1 million installs.

WP Super Cache

Install Now

A very fast caching engine for WordPress that produces static html files.

More Details

By Automattic

★ ★ ★ ★ ☆ (1,340)

Last Updated: 2 months ago

1+ Million Active Installations

✔ **Compatible** with your version of WordPress

When you visit a WordPress site, it actually talks to the site's database. It does that many times to collect all the information it needs to build a single page. With a caching plugin, WordPress will save the page so it doesn't need to get rebuilt every time.

However, in recent years, all of the high-quality WordPress hosting companies have developed their own caching solutions. This means that you probably don't need a caching plugin if you're using a good WordPress host.

So choosing a good hosting company with built-in caching is the most important choice you can make if you want a fast site.

Beyond the hosting, my other main recommendation is to make sure you don't slow down your site with large images. In the previous bonus chapter on Jetpack, we showed you how that plugin can optimize your images with the CDN and Lazy Load features. However, it is also worth spending some effort to make sure all your images are as lightweight as possible.

It's not unusual for people to upload images taken with a digital camera. Those images can often be over 5MB in size, and an image that big will always load really slowly.

So how can we make our images smaller? The plugin "Smush Image Compression and Optimization" will fix your oversize images.

Smush Image Compression and Optimization

Activate

More Details

Compress and optimize (or optimise) image files, improve performance and boost your SEO rank using Smush WordPress image compression and optimization.

By WPMU DEV

 (3,569)

Last Updated: 1 day ago

1+ Million Active Installations

✓ **Compatible** with your version of WordPress

- Install the Smush plugin, and you'll be offered three choices. I've enabled the first three options. I recommend enabling at least the first and third features on this list:

Automatically smush my images on upload

When you upload images to your site, Smush will automatically optimize them for you.

Preserve my image EXIF data

EXIF data stores camera settings, focal length, date, time and location information in image files. EXIF data makes image files larger but if you are a photographer you may want to preserve this information.

Resize my full size images

Set a maximum height and width for all images uploaded to your site so that any unnecessarily large images are automatically resized before they are added to the media gallery. This setting does not apply to images smushed using Directory Smush feature.

- After installing the plugin, WP Smush will look for images in your Media Library. Click "Bulk Smush" and your images will be as small as they can be while still looking good.

WP SMUSH

BULK SMUSH   Smush individual images via your Media Library

Steve, you have **18 attachments** that need smushing!

BULK SMUSH

MAKING SURE YOU CREATE GREAT CONTENT

If you have a lot of content on your WordPress site, it can be difficult to create consistent, high-quality product pages. With a lot of settings, its easy to forget something.

To make sure that all your WordPress content is created and organized in a way that meets your standards, we recommend the PublishPress plugin.

PublishPress – WordPress Content Calendar and Notification Workflows

Active

More Details

PublishPress is the collaboration tool WordPress teams. You get a beautiful editorial calendar and powerful...

By PublishPress

★ ★ ★ ★ ★ (14)

600+ Active Installations

Last Updated: 2 days ago

✓ **Compatible** with your version of WordPress

- Install the PublishPress plugin.
- The first screen you'll see is under "PublishPress" and then "Calendar". Here you'll see a calendar overview of all the content you've published on your site so far:

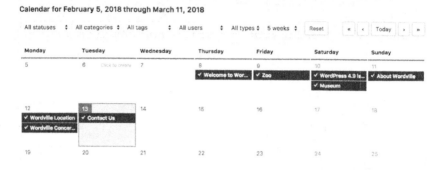

- If you want to plan new content, you can do that directly from this screen. Hover over a date and choose the "Click to create" option:

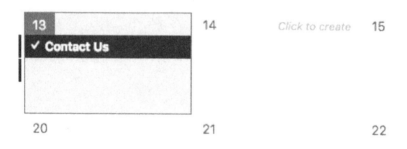

- You'll see a small pop-up box where you can plan the title and content for the new post:

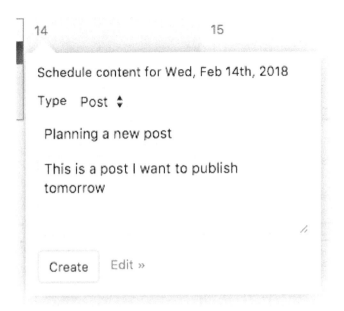

- You can drag-and-drop this post around the calendar if you want to move it to a different date. You'll also notice that planned and unpublished content is marked in green, rather than red. This makes it easy to see which content is in progress, and which content is already live on the site.

You can use PublishPress to plan your content. You can also use it to make sure all your content meets your standards.

- Buy and install the Content Checklist http://ostra.in/ checklist add-on.
- Go to "PublishPress" -> "Settings" -> "Checklist".

 **PublishPress**

Define tasks that must be complete before content is published

General	Calendar	Metadata	Statuses	User Groups	Checklist

- Check the "Post" box. This ensures that the Checklist feature will be used for Posts.

General:

Add to these post types: ☑ Post
☐ Page

- You can now choose all of your requirements for each post. You can choose the number of categories, tags, and words a post needs to have. You can decide whether people need to choose a featured image.

Requirements per Post Type:

Post   Page

Description	Action	Parameters	
Number of categories	Show a pop-up message ↕	Min 2	Max 5
Number of tags	Show a pop-up message ↕	Min 5	Max 10
Number of words	Show a pop-up message ↕	Min 200	Max 500
Featured image	Show a pop-up message ↕		
Excerpt has text	Disabled ↕		

Each requirement has a certain number of options:

- **Show a sidebar message** (default): This simply shows the recommendation in the sidebar when writing a WordPress post.

- **Show a pop-up message**: This will display a pop-up with a warning message, but users can still publish.

- **Prevent publishing**: Users won't be able to publish if this is not complete.

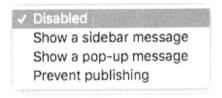

- Save the Checklist page.
- Go to edit a post, and check the new box in the right sidebar. Requirements that are complete have a green check. Requirement that are incomplete have a red X.

Checklist ▲

Visual   Text

✖ Between 2 and 5 categories

✖ Between 5 and 10 tags

✖ Between 200 and 500 words

✓ Featured image

On a busy site, the Content Checklist can save you from producing content that is too short, or doesn't meet your SEO standards. Particularly when combined with Yoast SEO, PublishPress can be a great asset when building WordPress sites.

CHAPTER 19.

BONUS: WORDPRESS ECOMMERCE EXPLAINED

In this chapter, we are going to take a look at eCommerce in WordPress.

WordPress is the most popular way to build a website. WooComemrce is the most popular way to build an eCommerce store. They make a great combination.

In this bonus chapter, we'll set up a small store where we can sell Wordville t-shirts. WooCommerce powers over 40% of all online stores. It's owned by a company called Automatic, the same company that runs WordPress.com and Jetpack.

The base plugin is free, but you can also buy extensions. The extensions range from $0 up to $249. The great thing is that WooCommerce is powerful enough out of the box that you probably won't need any extensions at all to get started.

- Log into your Wordville site and install the WooCommerce plugin. You may notice that if you search for "WooCommerce", it will find over 5,000 plugins related to WooCommerce. This is a *really* popular plugin!

- Immediately after installing it, you'll be taken to the WooCommerce onboarding wizard, which looks like the image below.

- Fill out your store's address – or your home office if you don't have a brick and mortar store.

- Choose your currency and what type of products you sell (digital or physical).

- At the bottom of the screen, there's a checkbox allowing WooCommerce to collect non-sensitive information about your store. If you leave this checked, your site will send WooCommerce information to make their software better.

- Click the purple "Let's go!" button to continue.

Store setup

The following wizard will help you configure your store and get you started quickly.

Where is your store based?
United States (US) — Florida

Address

Address line 2

City   Postcode / ZIP

What currency do you use?
United States dollar ($)

What type of product do you plan to sell?
I plan to sell both physical and digital products

☐ I will also be selling products or services in person.

☑ Allow WooCommerce to collect non-sensitive diagnostic data and usage information.

Let's go!

SETTING UP PAYMENT

On the next screen, you can choose how you want to get paid. WooCommerce offers a few options you can configure right now, and there are hundreds you can configure later.

WooCommerce presents two options (and offline payments like accepting checks):

- **Stripe**: http://ostra.in/woo-stripe
- **PayPal**: http://ostra.in/woo-paypal

These options might look pretty similar to someone who is just getting started. Let me try to simplify this for you:

- **Stripe** let's you accept credit cards.
- **PayPal** lets you accept credit cards and also PayPal payments.

For new store owners, I recommend using both Stripe and PayPal. I've used Stripe for years and I love their customer service, pricing, and their interface, so I'm definitely going to use Stripe with this site.

- The toggle for Stripe should already be set to "on" (purple). If you don't already have a Stripe account, you can check the box to automatically create an account for you.
- Make sure the toggle for PayPal is also on.
- Click "Continue" to move on to the next step.

Note: Depending on your location, you may see different payment options here. Ex. Stripe isn't available in all countries, so you may not see Stripe if you're not in a supported country. If that's the case, click the link for "Additional payment methods" to find a gateway you can use. You can do this after you finish the setup.

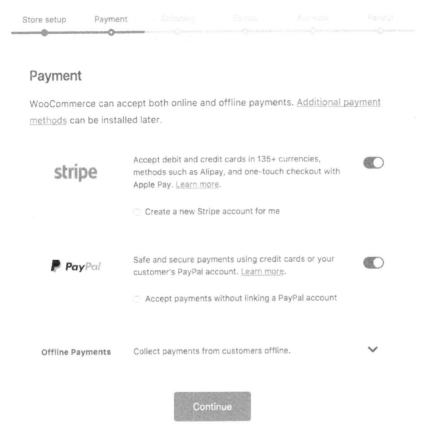

Payment

WooCommerce can accept both online and offline payments. Additional payment methods can be installed later.

stripe — Accept debit and credit cards in 135+ currencies, methods such as Alipay, and one-touch checkout with Apple Pay. Learn more.

☐ Create a new Stripe account for me

PayPal — Safe and secure payments using credit cards or your customer's PayPal account. Learn more.

☐ Accept payments without linking a PayPal account

Offline Payments — Collect payments from customers offline.

[Continue]

SETTING UP SHIPPING

The next screen is all about Shipping. You'll only see this if you are selling physical products. So if you selected "Digital Products" on the first screen, you'll skip this step.

You'll be prompted about *how* you want to ship your products. If you are based in the United States, you'll see "Live Rates" as the default method. That means your customers can choose a rate from USPS at checkout, and you as the store owner don't have to guesstimate a shipping cost. It's automatically calculated, and you can even print out a label at home. It's a *huge* time saver. Thus, I strongly recommend using live rates.

Note: If you select "Live Rates", WooCommerce will download the Jetpack plugin and install it for you automatically. Jetpack helps manage your connection to WordPress.com that provides this free service.

If you don't want to use Live Rates, or you don't live in the United States, you can select "Flat Rate" or "Free" – and for Flat Rate, you can enter your rate.

You'll also be prompted to select shipping units. These are determined by your location, so you most likely won't have to change this. WooCommerce correctly assumed I want to use ounces and inches for my store.

- Click "Continue" when you're done.

Shipping

You're all set up to ship anywhere in the United States (US), and outside of it. We recommend using **live rates** (which are powered by our WooCommerce Services plugin and Jetpack) to get accurate USPS shipping prices to cover the cost of order fulfillment.

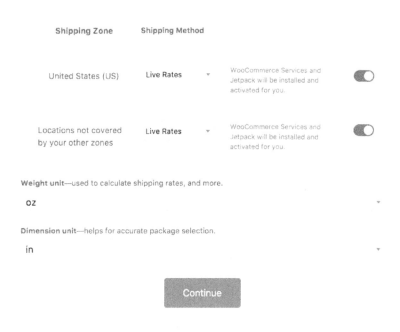

Shipping Zone	Shipping Method		
United States (US)	Live Rates ▾	WooCommerce Services and Jetpack will be installed and activated for you.	◉
Locations not covered by your other zones	Live Rates ▾	WooCommerce Services and Jetpack will be installed and activated for you.	◉

Weight unit—used to calculate shipping rates, and more.

OZ   ▾

Dimension unit—helps for accurate package selection.

in   ▾

Continue

SETTING UP EXTRAS

On the next page, you can enable two things, both of which I recommend.

- **Storefront Theme:** This is the recommended WooCommerce theme and is a great default theme. You can do a lot of customization with it. You can always switch at a later time to a different theme if you don't like Storefront.

- **Automated Taxes:** These are a huge deal for store owners. You want to get your store online and start making sales. You don't want to be fiddling with tax rates.

If you are using Live Rates for shipping, you already have all of the infrastructure in place. You can just turn on Automated Taxes and save yourself a lot of time.

- Click "Continue" when you're done.

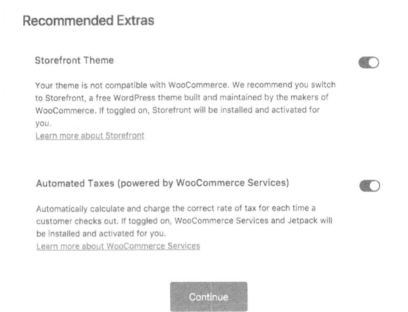

The last step in the onboarding wizard is to create a product. We're going to do that now. And we're going to add our first product to our store.

- Click "Create a product" to continue on to the next step.

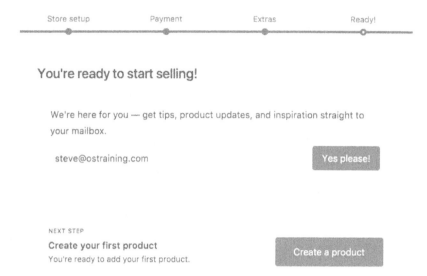

- You will now be on the "Add new product" page, as shown below.

- In the Title field, type in the name of the product: **Wordville T-Shirt**.

- In the description, type this: **This T-shirt has the Wordville logo and allows you to represent our great city.**

Add new product

Wordville T-Shirt

Permalink: http://wpexplained.com/product/wordville-t-shirt/ Edit

This T-shirt has the Wordville logo and allows you to represent our great city.

Below this Title and Description section, you'll see the "Product data" area. Here we can choose from a number of product types, such as simple products, grouped products, external/affiliate products and variable products.

For our example, we'll leave it as a simple product.

- Set the "Regular price" to 30.
- Set the "Sale price" to 25.

On the left-hand side of this area, you'll see several tabs. Click through to explore these options:

- **Inventory**: This is where you can enter the SKU number and tell WooCommerce whether or not this product is in stock. In the image below, we have 25 T-Shirts in stock:

- **Shipping**: Here we can choose the weight of the product.

You'll need to fill in the weight and dimensions if you want Live Shipping Rates. Go ahead and enter something in here if you aren't going to use Live Rates. That way you'll see where this information displays on the front end.

Product data —	Simple product	‡	Virtual:	Downloadable:		
✦ General	Weight (kg)		0.135			❷
◈ Inventory	Dimensions (cm)		73	43	2	❷
🚚 Shipping						
⬡ Linked Products	Shipping class		No shipping class		‡	❷
▣ Attributes						
⚙ Advanced						

- **Linked Products**: Here we can link this T-Shirt to other products, in the hope of encouraging people to buy more products, or higher-priced products. However, since this is our first product, we can't test this option yet.

- **Attributes**: If this T-Shirt came in different colors, we could use attributes and variations to display that to the user.

- **Advanced**: Here we can include a purchase note, a menu order, or disable reviews for the product.

ADDING A PRODUCT IMAGE

Just like WordPress posts, we can add a Featured Image to our WordPress product. However, since we are placing the image on a product page, we call it a "Product Image".

- Scroll down until you see "Product image" in the right sidebar.

- Click "Set product image".

- Open the Resources folder that you can download

from https://ostraining.com/books/wordpress/ resources. Upload the file called "wordville-tshirt.jpg".

- Click the "Set product image" button in the bottom right corner.

- Your new T-Shirt image will now appear in the right sidebar of your screen:

Click the image to edit or update

Remove product image

PUBLISHING THE PRODUCT

Let's publish the Wordville T-Shirt using the details we've entered so far.

- Scroll back to the top of the page and click the blue "Publish" button.

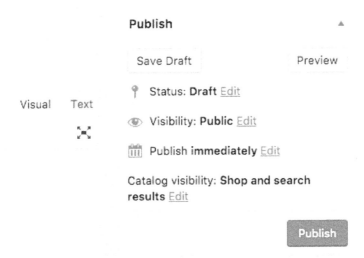

- Click the permalink under your product title. You'll see a screen similar to the one below. As you can see, we have the product title, price, description, product image, and the "Add to cart" button.

Home / Uncategorized / Wordville T-Shirt

Wordville T-Shirt

~~$30.00~~ **$25.00**

Availability: 25 in stock

| 1 | Add to cart |

Category: Uncategorized

Description   **Additional information**   **Reviews (0)**

This T-shirt has the Wordville logo and allows you to represent our great city.

- Click the "Add to cart" button.
- You'll see the message "'Wordville T-Shirt' has been added to your cart".
- Click "View cart".

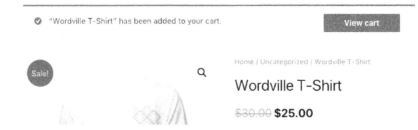

"Wordville T-Shirt" has been added to your cart.   View cart

Home / Uncategorized / Wordville T-Shirt

Wordville T-Shirt

~~$30.00~~ **$25.00**

- You'll now be taken to the "Cart" page of your store. Click "Proceed to checkout".

Cart

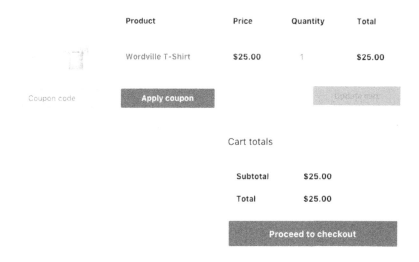

Product		Price	Quantity	Total
	Wordville T-Shirt	$25.00	1	$25.00

Coupon code	Apply coupon		Update cart

Cart totals

Subtotal	$25.00
Total	$25.00

Proceed to checkout

- You'll now be at the final checkout page. Here customers can enter their billing details and choose from any payment options that you have set up. Even if you don't have any payment options yet, you should still be able to click "Place Order" instead of "Continue to payment".

Checkout

☐ Have a coupon? Click here to enter your code

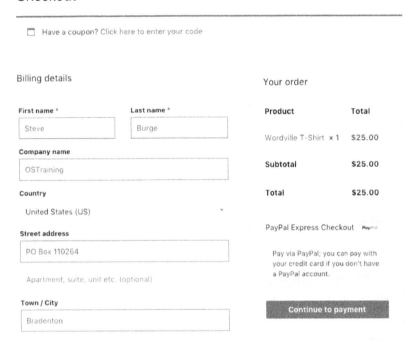

- Once an order has been placed, go back to your WordPress admin area.
- Click "WooCommerce" and then "Orders". You'll be able to see a list of all the orders placed in your new WooCommerce Store!

Hopefully this introductory chapter gives you a taste of how easy WooCommerce can be to use. We didn't have the space to start exploring all of WooCommerce's features, but trust me – it can be powerful as well as easy.

If you want to learn more about WooCommerce, check out the WooCommerce Explained book: https://ostraining.com/books/woocommerce.

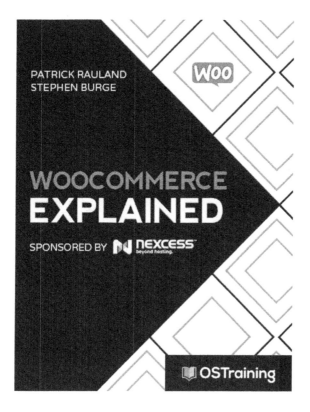

Made in the USA
Coppell, TX
11 May 2020